The Aftermath of Battle

THE BURIAL OF THE CIVIL WAR DEAD

Meg Groeling

EMERGING CIVIL WAR SERIES

Chris Mackowski, series editor
Daniel T. Davis, chief historian
Kristopher D. White, emeritus editor

The Emerging Civil War Series:

THE BURIAL OF
THE CIVIL WAR DEAD

Meg Groeling

EMERGING CIVIL WAR SERIES

SB

Savas Beatie

California

First edition, first printing

ISBN-13: 978-1-61121-189-4; eISBN: 978-1-61121-190-0

Library of Congress Control Number: 2014958444

SB

Published by
Savas Beatie LLC
989 Governor Drive, Suite 102
El Dorado Hills, California 95762
Phone: 916-941-6896
Email: sales@savasbeatie.com
Web: www.savasbeatie.com

Savas Beatie titles are available at special discounts for bulk purchases in the United States by corporations, institutions, and other organizations. For more details, please contact Special Sales, P.O. Box 4527, El Dorado Hills, CA 95762, or you may e-mail us as at sales@savasbeatie.com, or visit our website at www.savasbeatie.com for additional information.

For my Dad

Table of Contents

The graves at Vicksburg National Cemetery write themselves across the landscape like Braille. (cm)

Footnotes for this volume are available at
http://emergingcivilwar.com/publications/the-emerging-civil-war-series/footnotes

Acknowledgments

Sometimes a person just has to wait for the best to finally show up. Thank you to all the fine folks at *Emerging Civil War*, especially Daniel Davis and Chris Mackowski. Both have done yeoman work editing this book, and Chris has been my Number One Fan from the beginning. Savas Beatie would never know of my existence if not for *ECW*. Thanks for this opportunity. Thanks especially to Theodore Savas.

The staff at Brownell Middle School, in Gilroy, California, has been very understanding as I transition from math teacher to historian. The discipline of mathematics has made me a better thinker all around. Thanks to Greg Camacho-Light, my principal, and Pat Rogers, my department chair. Both have provided an environment wherein reaching for the moon and stars is simply a daily occurrence.

Dr. Steven Woodworth graciously read the text of *Aftermath* as part of one of my American Public University classes. His help and encouragement on all fronts has been invaluable. Thank you to all who read parts of my manuscript, especially Chris Kolakowski, Paul Perreault, and Jari Villaneuva, without whom I would have even less of an understanding about topics naval, environmental, and musical.

Thanks to the many people who contributed photographs to this book. Thanks, too, to Kris White, who has been patient with me since Day One at ECW.

My family has always been supportive, especially my sister, Martha. She never lets me do less than my best. My little tuxedo cat, MaryCATherine, never fails to run to the office to keep me company when it is time to write. That cat knows more about the American Civil War than any animal has a right to know!

And finally, thanks to my husband Robert Groeling, who has stood by my side for a while now, reminding me that I am worthy of love and support. For that I can only return the favor, tenfold.

THANK YOU ALL. Huzzah!

At Bentonville Battlefield State Historical Site, a monument to North Carolina's soldiers depicts the grieving loved ones back home. (cm)

A lone cannon sits amidst the graves at Stones River National Cemetery. (cm)

A Note About the Text

This study is based upon a wide variety of sources, available for review in the footnotes found at http://emergingcivilwar.com/publications/the-emerging-civil-war-series/footnotes. I decided, however, to utilize some of the source material apocryphally in a few of the chapter introductions in an effort to set a particular mood and establish a certain tone. Instances of theses brief clips of creative license are likewise identified in the footnotes.

For the Emerging Civil War Series

Theodore P. Savas, *publisher*
Chris Mackowski, *series editor and co-founder*
Daniel T. Davis, *chief historian*
Sarah Keeney, *editorial consultant*
Kristopher D. White, *emeritus editor and co-founder*   Design and layout by Chris Mackowski

Foreword

"What did they do with all the bodies?"

Those of us who regularly give battlefield tours have all had visitors who've asked us that question. After we've explained the action on the field, visitors struggle to wrap their heads around the scale of the carnage. Most shake their heads, but occasionally someone understands that the story they've just heard represents not just a tragic loss of life but a terrible, *immediate* logistical problem, too.

Even to this day, scholars actively debate the actual number of deaths attributed to the war. For decades, the accepted number was 620,000, although more recent studies have expanded that number to be from anywhere between 650,000 to 850,000 men. Such numbers are so huge as to be abstract.

It's little wonder, then, that *more* people don't ask about the dead. Instead, visitors tend to concentrate on their heroes or their ancestors—the men whose footsteps they can follow across the battlefields. Unfortunately, many men forever stayed on those same fields. In some places, there are men doubtlessly still out there. That's why we refer to such places as "hallowed ground."

This is the story of those men who stayed behind—those hundreds of thousands of men—and what happened to them.

— Chris Mackowski
 Editor

"After the battle, what did they do with all the bodies?"
— *common question from battlefield visitors*

The First to Fall

PROLOGUE

MAY 24, 1861

The morning of May 24, 1861, came early in those pre-daylight savings times, about 4:45 a.m. A short, older man walked the dirt streets of Mechanicville, New York, to the local New York and Western Union telegraph office. Mr. Ephraim Ellsworth was alone, his feet making soft indentions on the new spring grass that grew by the side of the road. His wife was still in bed. Phebe suffered from Parkinson's disease, worse now than it had ever been.

Their son, Elmer, was supposed to be in a battle today. At least they thought it was a battle—no one was sure. All they really knew was that Elmer, at the head of his brigade of New York Zouave firefighters, was to cross the Potomac River from Washington, D.C., and enter the Virginia town of Alexandria. The crossing was at night, under a full moon. Whether that augured well or poorly was still to be seen. The whole Federal army was to be in on the movement, but more specific news had been scarce this far away from the capital.

Mr. Ellsworth sat, waiting. The telegraph whirred and clicked throughout the early morning, then one of the operators suddenly gasped and burst into tears. He looked up at Mr. Ellsworth, rose, and walked to him, holding a piece of paper. The operator's hand shook as he handed the Western Union onionskin to the waiting father. Mr. Ellsworth looked at the words, not trusting himself to read or understand their message. By the second reading, however, the communication was clear: their son, Elmer, was dead.

Shocked and shaken, Ephraim Ellsworth walked slowly back to the low-browed cottage. Now what? First

ABOVE: With his hat askew at a jaunty angle, young Elmer Ellsworth had a bit of swashbuckle about him. (mg)

OPPOSITE: The author's collection of Ellsworth memorabilia demonstrates the wide appeal the martyred Ellsworth had as an icon. (mg)

DEATH OF COL. ELLSWORTH.

TOP: Ellsworth's death became iconic and made him a martyr. ABOVE: Francis Brownell later posed with his bayonet-tipped rifle, with Ellsworth's captured flag draped near his feet. (loc)
(loc)

he must tell Phebe that their handsome, charismatic 24-year-old son was gone—forever gone—from their lives. His merry hazel eyes and authoritative voice were stilled, his idealistic letters silenced. His high-flown dreams of a career commanding men would never be a reality. A shotgun shell extinguished much of the happiness of their lives. How? Where? Why

Should they go get Elmer's body? Was there a body to get? How was it supposed to be shipped to New York, to be buried in Mechanicville? What were parents of a soldier supposed to do legally? Who had seen him last? Did he suffer or go quickly? What were his last thoughts? Last words? How were he and Phebe supposed to face the rest of their lives without him? So many unanswered questions. . . .

Ellsworth had been killed in Alexandria, Virginia, that morning—the victim of a fight but not of battle. He and a small group of soldiers and reporters were coming down a flight of stairs from the roof of the Marshall House hotel, where they had just removed a large Confederate flag belonging to the hotel's proprietor, James Jackson. Ellsworth carried the flag. Jackson shot him through the heart with one barrel of a shotgun. Before Jackson was able to discharge the second barrel, Cpl. Francis Brownell deflected the weapon and discharged his own, killing Jackson immediately.

Ephraim and Phebe Ellsworth would not mourn their son's death alone. The entire North would support them in their sorrow, as the loss of Ellsworth was a national tragedy. Their son, Col. Elmer Ellsworth, was the first Union officer to die in the American Civil War. Flags were lowered to half-staff in Washington, D.C., and President Lincoln ordered that Ellsworth's body was to lie in state in the White House. Lincoln himself wrote to the Ellsworths, in solidarity with their sadness. The funeral train, draped with black and flying the national flag, passed from Washington to New York City, then up the Hudson River. Eight men from Colonel Ellsworth's regiment, the 11th New York Fire Zouaves, accompanied the remains and comforted the bereaved parents. They stayed with their commander across upstate New York, where he was interred in Hudson View Cemetery. Later, in the silence, the cicadas would sing their requiem.

No one realized at the time that within a few weeks, such a burial would be a near impossibility. Telegrams announcing the deaths of other sons, North and South, would become all too common. Many deaths occurred in which no one could be notified. Soldier after soldier was buried in an anonymous trench or left to rot somewhere on the battlefield. More dead piled up—in mass graves, in unknown places, at the bottoms of creeks, rivers, and oceans, burned to death in the Wilderness, starved, frozen, dead by disease. Cannon fire broke bodies into molecules, never to be recovered. Mass graves contained soldiers from both sides of the conflict, and there was no DNA to help identify anyone. Hospital graveyards grew enormous, and new cemeteries were created in both the North and the South. To a single family, only one death was mourned. The national family eventually mourned the loss of more than 750,000 men.

Ellsworth lay in state in the White House, mourned by his good friend, Abraham Lincoln. (loc)

Elmer Ellsworth is now known only for being the first officer to die in battle in the Civil War. His blood was among the first drops shed in what came to be a deluge, touching in some manner almost every family in America. *Aftermath of Battle* is a book about the hundreds of thousands more who gave their last full measure in the worst of America's wars. The places and episodes in this book have been chosen with the hope that, by telling their stories, the reader will get an overarching view of the evolution of thought and action concerning the remains of the Civil War dead. National cemeteries, private burying grounds, Unknown Soldier tombs, and Memorial Days— this book attempts to answer the question, "What did they do with all the bodies?"

Envelopes emblazoned with scenes from Ellsworth's martyrdom became forms of early war propaganda. (loc)

Many a One of Us Will be Cold Tomorrow Night

CHAPTER ONE

JULY 21, 1861

On July 20, 1861, tall, bearded Pvt. Arthur Alcock walked the makeshift campgrounds of the 11th New York Fire Zouaves at Centerville. He had arrived about 10:00 p.m. after obtaining hospital supplies at Alexandria

for the regimental surgeon, Dr. Charles Gray. Alcock visited the officers of the different units, getting a cup of coffee and a roasted potato from Capt. Michael Tagan of Company D along with some good conversation from the sleepless men. Each one knew that the next day would bring a fight, the Fire Zouaves' first one. The "bespangled sons of Mars," now weary, footsore, and hungry, contemplated their immediate future. Lieutenant Daniel Diver, who did not know that he was enjoying his last night alive, accompanied Alcock in his ramble.

The two men discussed the condition of the troops, commenting on their good spirits "in view of the expected fight" the next day. In Alcock's journal, written during his imprisonment in Richmond after the first battle of Bull Run, wrote, "poor Diver said to me, 'Many a one of us will be cold to-morrow night.' Who will say that 'coming events *do not* cast their shadows before?'"

Before the third week in July, Union and Confederate armies had prepared somewhat for the sad fact that the coming altercation would probably result in casualties of some variety. The firing on Fort Sumter three months earlier was an anomaly; it had produced no deaths attributable to the actual fighting. No one was naive enough to think this trend would continue, so the Federals prepared hospitals in Washington, D.C., for incoming wounded. Wagons were equipped to carry

ABOVE: The distinctive uniforms of the Zouaves—such as the one on display at the Fredericksburg Battlefield Visitor Center—were based on a French design. (cm)

OPPOSITE: The 2nd Rhode Island Infantry came to grief on Matthews Hill at Manassas. (cm)

medical supplies to the field of battle, and the Union had purchased both two- and four-wheeled varieties to be used as ambulances; the larger one would return to the capital with wounded who had been triaged on the scene. The Confederacy brought similar wagons, planning to evacuate its wounded to hospitals in and around Richmond. On both sides, women staffed these makeshift facilities.

A walking trail across Matthews Hill follows part of the Federal advance, which came from the right of the photo toward the fence. Somewhere in this area on Matthews Hill, the 2nd Rhode Island Infantry lost its officers. (ro)

No one had really thought what to do with any dead men that might actually accrue during the brief kerfuffle. After all, one Confederate could easily whip from three to 10 Yankees; or, if one preferred, one Yankee just had to stand his ground and the blustering Rebels would run out of things to brag about and retreat. It would be one short, decisive battle, and then the war would be over— or so many thought.

The first battle of Bull Run, also known as First Manassas, was fought on July 21, 1861, near the city of Manassas, Virginia, not far from the Federal capital in Washington. It was the first major battle of the Civil War. Union forces fought well early in the day, but the Confederate forces, strengthened by reinforcements that arrived by rail, eventually won the battle. Each side had about 30,000 inexperienced troops led by equally inexperienced officers. The Confederate victory was followed by a disorganized Union retreat.

In hindsight, the casualties were light, at least compared to what the future held. Approximately 400 Confederates were killed and 1,600 wounded. Union forces had comparable casualty rates: 460 killed and 1,124 wounded, with an additional 1,312 Union soldiers listed as missing and captured. Even at the time, Massachusetts Senator Henry Wilson referred to it as a "tupenny skirmish," but these deaths deeply affected communities in 20 states, both Northern and Southern. The majority of casualties were from either New York or Virginia. Now, as one Virginian said, "War was no longer funny."

Both Union and Confederate dead lay exposed to a terrible rainstorm that began the evening of the 21st and continued all the next day. Federal troops had rather abruptly left the battlefield, being unceremoniously routed by the Confederates after several hours of intense fighting during which the outcome of the battle was uncertain. At the end, however, it *was* certain—the Federal forces had lost the first engagement of the war.

Private Alcock was the orderly for Dr. Gray, the regimental surgeon for the 11th New York Fire Zouaves. Due to his position as a non-combatant, he was able to observe his surroundings, and he gave his report later on, in the journal he wrote in prison. Dr. Gray and several other surgeons had set up a field hospital at the Sudley Methodist Church, on the upper northwest part of the battlefield. As the battle wound down outside the little church, Alcock and the others realized that, although they were in

danger of becoming prisoners, they could not stop their bloody work. "In the church," Alcock wrote, "the scene of human suffering was terrible. Every part of the floor was covered with the wounded—dying and dead. . . . So close together did the wounded lay upon the floor, that it was with the greatest I could pick my way through them."

Cries of "Water, water, for God's sake!" and "Oh! For Heaven's sake don't step on me," rang everywhere. No amount of pleading on the parts of the doctors, their assistants, or the wounded kept the Confederate cavalry lieutenant in charge of rounding up prisoners in that part of the field from forcing all who could walk, regardless of situation, to begin the eight mile trek to Manassas. Many men were left behind, and the little group of Federals "passed by scores of dead men and horses, many of them horribly mutilated." The grim work of burial would begin almost immediately, even in the rain.

Usually burial work was the job of slaves, but there were far too many bodies for the few slaves available in the Manassas-Centerville area to bury them quickly. This was the first battle, after all, and sometimes a friend or brother wanted to perform this service for those about whom he cared. One Confederate soldier decided he would go back to the battlefield to find his friend Blue.

Judith Henry, too infirm to evacuate her home during the battle, became the first civilian casualty of the Civil War when an artillery shell exploded in her bedroom, killing her. After the battle, her family buried her in a small plot behind the house, where visitors to the battlefield can still pay their respects. (cm)

Battlefield visitors look for remains on the Manassas battlefield; through the trees, Sudley Church stands on the ridge in the background. (loc)

After he located Blue's body, he used a hoe and a spade to dig a grave in the orchard next to Mrs. Henry's house. As he worked, another Confederate came up to him and asked to borrow the tools, as he had located his brother's remains and wished to bury him as well. The rain poured down over the two men and their sad burdens, so the two agreed to work together to dig a hole large enough to accommodate both dead men. "So we buried them that way," the first soldier recalled, "and gathered up some old shingles to put over the bodies."

Because the Confederates had won the battle, they were left in charge of the field. The burials were done hastily, with little attention to detail, and within three days the field was considered cleared, although a spot of rain might uncover a decomposing foot or hand. The dead, however, did not necessarily rest in peace.

*   *   *

Many men who died at the First Bull Run have become famous and their remains are identified and well-cared for. Confederate Gen. Barnard Bee, who gave Brigade Commander Thomas Jackson his sobriquet "Stonewall," and Confederate Col. Francis Bartow, who died after having been hit in the chest by a projectile while leading Col. Lucius J. Gartrell's 7th Georgians up Henry House Hill, are two examples. Bee's and Bartow's remains were taken back to Richmond via train, given services at St. Paul's Episcopal Church, and then sent to their families for burial.

Union Maj. Sullivan Ballou, of the 2nd Rhode Island, and arguably the most romantic man in either army, was not so lucky. He and several other Rhode Island officers had been too badly injured to move during the Union

A monument to Col. John Slocum (above) was erected by the Grand Army of the Republic at Swan Point Cemetery in Providence, Rhode Island. (mg)

Sullivan Ballou (below) gained national attention for modern audiences when Ken Burns featured him at the end of the first episode of his 1990 film *The Civil War*. Ballou wrote a poignant letter to his wife, Sarah, just days before being killed at the battle of First Manassas.

"The indications are very strong that we shall move in a few days—perhaps tomorrow. Lest I should not be able to write you again, I feel impelled to write lines that may fall under your eye when I shall be no more. . . .

"If it is necessary that I should fall on the battlefield for my country, I am ready. I have no misgivings about, or lack of confidence in, the cause in which I am engaged, and my courage does not halt or falter. I know how strongly American Civilization now leans upon the triumph of the Government, and how great a debt we owe to those who went before us through the blood and suffering of the Revolution. And I am willing—perfectly willing—to lay down all my joys in this life, to help maintain this Government, and to pay that debt. . . .

"I cannot describe to you my feelings on this calm summer night, when two thousand men are sleeping around me, many of them enjoying the last, perhaps, before that of death—and I, suspicious that Death is creeping behind me with his fatal dart, am communing with God, my country, and thee. . . .

"Sarah, my love for you is deathless, it seems to bind me to you with mighty cables that nothing but Omnipotence could break; and yet my love of Country comes over me like a strong wind and bears me irresistibly on with all these chains to the battlefield. . . .

"And hard it is for me to give them up and burn to ashes the hopes of future years, when God willing, we might still have lived and loved together and seen our sons grow up to honorable manhood around us. . . . If I do not, my dear Sarah, never forget how much I love you, and when my last breath escapes me on the battlefield, it will whisper your name.

"Forgive my many faults, and the many pains I have caused you. How thoughtless and foolish I have oftentimes been! How gladly would I wash out with my tears every little spot upon your happiness, and struggle with all the misfortune of this world, to shield you and my children from harm. But I cannot. I must watch you from the spirit land and hover near you, while you buffet the storms with your precious little freight, and wait with sad patience till we meet to part no more.

"But, O Sarah! If the dead can come back to this earth and flit unseen around those they loved, I shall always be near you; in the garish day and in the darkest night—amidst your happiest scenes and gloomiest hours—always, always; and if there be a soft breeze upon your cheek, it shall be my breath; or the cool air fans your throbbing temple, it shall be my spirit passing by.

"Sarah, do not mourn me dead; think I am gone and wait for thee, for we shall meet again. . . ."

Rhode Island's 29-year-old chief executive, William Sprague, referred to himself as "The Boy Governor." While serving in office, he participated in the battle of First Manassas, serving as an aide to home-state hero Ambrose Burnside. (mg)

retreat, and were left at the field hospital within Sudley Church. The men were then moved to the Thornberry house, where Rhode Island Col. John S. Slocum died on July 23 and Ballou on the 28th. They were buried, side-by-side, near Sudley Church. Rumors had surfaced in the winter of 1861 that some Confederates had returned to the battlefield and exhumed Federal bodies, the Rhode Island officers being among those who were desecrated. Rhode Island Governor William Sprague and his party of 70 politicians and soldiers left Washington, D.C., on the rainy morning of March 19, 1862, to check the truth of the rumors and retrieve the bodies of their officers and men, if possible.

Progress was slow, and the Boy Governor of Rhode Island and his friends reached the battlefield on March 21. They were unable to find the graves they sought, although they did come upon a skeleton leaning against a tree. The skeleton was unable to offer much information, and the group continued across Bull Run to the now-abandoned Sudley Church. Sprague directed his secretary, Walter Coleman, to begin digging at two burial mounds that had been identified as belonging to Slocum and Ballou. (The rest of the story gets awful, and it can be found in the *Reports* of the Joint Committee of the Conduct of the War, Volume 3, pp. 458-460.)

Dr. Greely was sworn in by the committee and examined by its chairman. He was asked the purpose for his being on the field at that time, and he explained that he and the rest of Governor Sprague's party were looking for the remains of Rhode Island officers:

> *[T]his colored girl came down where they were and asked them what they were digging for. Said she, "if you are digging for the body of Colonel Sloke—,". . . One of the party said "Colonel Slocum." "Yes, sir," said she, "that is the name; you won't find him ; the Georgia regiment men dug him up some weeks ago, and first cut off his head and then burned his body in the little hollow there," pointing it out to us. She told us that his shirts were down in a place that she pointed out, and that his coffin had been left in the stream . . .*

Another child corroborated the girl's story, and added that it was the 21st Georgia who burned the body and left with its skull. Acting on this information, several of the men went down to the little streambed. They easily found where a fire had been lit, and within the fire pit were several human bones. There was no portion of a skull, although the ashes were examined with care.

The rest of the party continued to look for the graves of Slocum and Ballou. Nothing had been found until Greely suggested running a sabre into the ground. If a coffin were buried there, the sabre would indicate its presence. In this manner the remains of Slocum were found and identified by his uniform. There was no sign of Ballou's body at the gravesite. Greely and the other men inferred that the bone fragments must be those of Ballou, and that the Georgia regiment had taken his skull away.

Governor William Sprague and the Reverend Frederick Denison corroborated Dr. Greeley's appalling testimony. The 21st Georgia, for revenge, had mutilated the body of a Federal

officer, attempted to burn the body itself, and took the head with them when they left the area, believing it to be that of Col. Henry Slocum. It belonged, however, to Maj. Sullivan Ballou. Whether it became a drinking cup is not known, although rumors persisted throughout the entire war of just such atrocities.

While the exact location of Ballou's body may never be known, some historians believe it's somewhere near the Thornberry house. (ro)

The Federal government quickly realized that something must be put in place to standardize burial practices after a battle. Secretary of War Simon Cameron issued General Order No. 75 on September 11, 1861. This order stated that forms should be printed and available in every general and post hospital to preserve "accurate and permanent records of the deceased." Copies of mortuary records were to be forwarded to the adjutant-general in Washington. Additionally, each quartermaster was ordered to provide a registered headboard, "to be secured at the head of each soldier's grave." Of course, nothing ever goes as planned, especially in war. It was not until the slaughters of Shiloh and Antietam that the government created standards for the acceptance of surgeons and other medical personnel into the armed forces (General Order No. 43) and defining the official duties of chief medical officers in the field or in a hospital setting (General Order No. 36). Even these did not help much—chaos, terror, and death are not very good about filling out their forms in triplicate.

At Manassas National Battlefield

The Manassas Battlefield Visitor Center sits atop Henry Hill (above), in the heart of the action that tipped the balance of the fight in favor of the Confederates. A second visitor center that focuses primarily on the battle of Second Manassas is located a little to the west at the Brawner farm. (cm)

A visitor gets two-for-one at the National Battlefield Park of Manassas, since two battles took place at this site—or three-for-one, if you are a bird-watcher. The National Audubon Society has designated the Manassas Battlefield Park as an Important Bird Area.

The Henry Hill Visitor Center is next to the parking lot, and is wheelchair-accessible. As a general rule, the park is open every day except Thanksgiving and Christmas, but phone ahead or check the NPS website for specific information: www.nps.gov/mana/index.htm. There is a Park Orientation Film, "Manassas: End of Innocence," that is shown hourly and is free. It is close-captioned, and hearing assisted devices are available upon request. The Visitor Center displays artifacts and exhibits pertaining to the first battle of Bull Run/ Manassas. There is a fiber-optic battle map, as well, to give visitors an overview of the troop movements during the battle. The bookstore is terrific, for those of you who consider this the most important part of the experience, but then, all NPS bookstores are wonderlands of souvenirs items, collectibles, art prints, reproductions, music CDs, movie DVDs, and, of course, books about the battle and the Civil War in general.

Ranger-led walks are available in many formats, from short and kid-friendly programs around the visitor center to longer treks to specific areas. Hikes vary from the 1.1 mile Henry Hill Loop Trail to the longer First Manassas Loop rail (5.4 miles) and the Second Manassas Loop (6.2 miles). There is a 20-mile driving tour that is self-guided and takes two to three hours to compete. There are also 21 miles of trails within the park that are designated equestrian trails, but you must bring your own horse.

The closer the date of a visit is to the date of the battle, the greater the chance of seeing Living History demonstrations and battle commemorations.

If one wishes to see the area where Major Ballou's body was burned, ask a Park Service employee for assistance.

There are electronic battle apps for First and Second Manassas, and these provide detailed overviews of each engagement. Seasonal exhibits such as the Stone House and the Brawner Farm Interpretive Center (which interprets the time period of Second Manassas) are open at designated times. The schedules are subject to change without notice due to weather and staffing, so please check ahead of time to see exactly what will be available for you when you come to this outstanding battlefield park.

For GPS devices, the mailing address of the Henry Hill Visitor Center is: 6511 Sudley Road, Manassas, VA, 20109. There is no public transportation to the park.

At Sudley Methodist Church

The small church that served as a field hospital during the first battle of Bull Run is not a museum. It is an active, well-attended Methodist church, with Vacation Bible School and Sunday Worship.

To pay a visit to Sudley Methodist, travel along the Sudley Road to the north-west corner of the Manassas Park Battlefield to 5308 Sudley Road. It is on the left side. Access their website to find out when services are scheduled, or to read more about this tiny little plot of history: www.sudley-methodist.org.

The modern Sudley Methodist Church, still an active congregation, sits on the site of the wartime church. (ro)

Rooting Hogs and Angel's Glow

CHAPTER TWO

APRIL 6-7, 1862

Confederate Pvt. Henry M. Stanley of the 6th Arkansas Infantry was a reluctant soldier. Tall, thin, only 21 years old in April of 1862, he firmly denied his Welsh ancestry to his messmates, preferring them to think he was native born. He hated that he had the star-crossed background of illegitimacy and poverty. The young, mustachioed private kept to himself and only shared his thoughts with his diary.

As his unit marched through the northwestern area of Tennessee in the early morning, the soldier noted the thin forest and the withered grass not yet ready to shake off its winter hues. The sun gradually rose. It warmed the men and helped Henry settle his thoughts. He decided the woods looked like a "grand place for a picnic," but considered it strange that there might be a battle on a Sunday, disturbing the "holy calm" of the vicinity.

Later, Stanley would go on to fame as the erstwhile explorer tasked with finding Dr. David Livingston, lost somewhere in the interior of Africa, but he was also a soldier at Shiloh, captured at the end of April 6, 1862, by the "terrible Yankees." The "holy calm" of the woods around Pittsburg Landing would not be "a grand place for a picnic" for a very long time.

The battle of Shiloh, also known as the battle of Pittsburgh Landing, was fought April 6-7, 1862, in southwestern Tennessee. Major General Ulysses S. Grant commanded the Union forces. He had moved his army via the Tennessee River deep into Tennessee and was encamped on the west bank of the river, at Pittsburgh Landing. It was here that Confederate forces under Gens. Albert Sydney Johnston and P. G. T. Beauregard launched a surprise attack on Grant's army early on the morning of the sixth. The Confederates achieved

Historians have identified twelve mass Confederate graves on the Shiloh battlefield, although only five of them have been formally marked. (cm)

considerable success on the first day, but were ultimately defeated on the second day.

Shiloh has the unsavory reputation of being the deadliest engagement in American history up to that

time. Union casualties were 13,047 (1,754 killed, 8,408 wounded, and 2,885 missing) and Confederate casualties were 10,699 (1,728 killed, 8,012 wounded, and 959 missing or captured.) The dead included the Confederate army's Gen. Albert Sidney Johnston; the highest-ranking Union officer to die was division commander W. H. L. Wallace—two dead officers, but almost 3,500 other men died as well.

While more than 1,725 Confederates were killed during the battle of Shiloh, the death of Gen. Albert Sydney Johnston—the highest-ranking Confederate killed during the war—had far-reaching implications. Johnston's death gave rise to one of the central tenets of the Lost Cause: the "Lost Opportunity." Johnston's successor, Gen. P. G. T. Beauregard, ordered a retreat on the second day of the battle, thus squandering Johnston's gains from the day before. While not grounded in fact, the premise has been a favorite source of "What If?" speculations for Lost Cause apologists ever since. (cm)

And because the battle lasted as long as it did, there was more than one terrible aftermath.

* * *

Anchored to the docks at Pittsburg Landing were hospital ships, sent to aid the Union army by private individuals, states, and the army itself. Not all these ships had a doctor or a nurse aboard to help the wounded. Many were sent to carry casualties to places of safety. One of these was the steamer *Continental*. Wounded were brought aboard all through the afternoon and evening of April 6, and a more perfect ship of horrors cannot be imagined. "So numerous were the dead, dying, and wounded that a person could scarcely move without stepping on them . . ." wrote a wounded young Iowan who served in Brig. Gen. Stephen A. Hurlbut's Division. "[M]angled in every conceivable way . . . some with arms, legs, and even their jaws shot off, bleeding to death, and no one to wait upon them or dress their wounds."

The only certified hospital boat, the *City of Memphis*, carried its sad, gruesome cargo back and forth to Savannah, Tennessee, without a pause, refueling as the wounded and dead were loaded and unloaded.

It was much worse for those still ashore. With few doctors, and very little medical supplies on either side, the sheer number of wounded and dead overwhelmed both armies. They all lay there, in the evening drizzle and in the torrential rains later in the night. One drummer boy from an Illinois regiment was so exhausted, physically and emotionally, that he finally just dropped where he stood, near a little log house. When he awoke, he discovered that, in his deep slumber, he had been mistaken for a corpse. Horribly, he was now lying at the head of a grisly row of dead men waiting for burial.

Those who lay among the carnage were about to endure a seemingly unending nightmare. Wherever there are woods and water, there are scavenger animals, even now.—One of the most frightening was the feral pig. Whether a relative of European boars or just local pigs gone wild, a feral pig was a ferocious predator, and the dead and injured of Shiloh provided quite a feast for these cannibal rototillers. They were poor at discriminating between really dead and just badly wounded, so they ate Union and Confederate casualties indiscriminately.

The diary of an exhausted Confederate soldier on night patrol painted an unforgettable picture of horror. "Vivid flashings of lightning rent the havens and . . . sickening sights fell before my eyes . . ." he wrote. "I saw a large piece of ground literally covered with dead heaped and piled upon each other. I shut my eyes upon the sickening sight. . . . Through the dark I heard the sound of hogs quarreling over their carnival feast."

Men lying on the battlefield could hear feral pigs munching on Union and Confederate soldiers, raiding the arm-and-leg piles around the field hospitals, grunting and rooting around in human remains—and the wounded men were helpless to defend themselves. Considering the fear of being eaten alive by feral pigs, in the driving night rain, listening to all the sickening sounds of men hurt and dying, and that the natural lightning was amplified by Grant's orders to Union gunboats *Lexington* and *Tyler* to continue harassing the enemy by shelling Confederate positions throughout the night—it is difficult to imagine a more horrifying set of circumstances.

When Union Gen. Don Carlos Buell's men arrived at the landing to reinforce Gen. Ulysses Grant's demoralized soldiers, one of them wrote, "I think I give the experience of every member of [my regiment] . . . when I say that the night of the 6th if April, 1862, was the worst night of our entire three years service."

A replica of Shiloh church stands in the location of the wartime structure. "Shiloh" means "place of peace." (cm)

*   *   *

The next day, Grant roused his troops from utter exhaustion and attacked the Confederates, now under the command of Beauregard. Reeling from events of the day before, the rebels fought piecemeal and finally retreated toward Corinth in an unending downfall of rain. "Every house between here [Corinth] and the battlefield is a hospital," one Tennessee soldier wrote, "and the whole road is lined with wagons freighted with dead and wounded."

On April 8, Beauregard had sent an official message to Grant requesting permission to send, under a flag of truce, a "mounted party to the battle-field of Shiloh for the purpose of giving decent interment to my dead." Grant answered the Confederate commander as soon as he received the message. "Owing to the warmth of the weather I deemed it advisable to have all the dead of both parties buried immediately," he wrote. "Heavy details were made for this purpose, and it is now accomplished." No other help was necessary, he said, adding, "I shall always be glad to extend any courtesy consistent with duty, and especially so when dictated by humanity."

The Confederate troops continued in their misery through April 9. Makeshift hospitals had sprung up all over Corinth, but there was no medicine, no edible meat, and not a drop of alcohol or morphine to ease the pain of any type of operation. Doctors began to furlough patients who were mobile enough to leave the area. It was not until Confederate Gen. Earl Van Dorn arrived with his men from the trans-Mississippi in mid-April that the Confederate army was able to feel truly safe.

*   *   *

The victor of a battle is tasked with cleaning up the battlefield, and the job of cleaning up after Shiloh as Grant had ordered loomed large. This level of destruction had never been seen before in North America. "As far as the eye could reach, in every direction, lay the silent forms of those who went down before the storm of battle," wrote one of Buell's soldiers. One of the men who served in W. H. L. Wallace's division noted, "I could have walked across that field on dead Rebels, they were so thick, and all were as black as could be—a most sickening sight."

Shiloh is relatively unique in that the Confederate dead still remain on the battlefield. Grant's order of April 8 applied to both sides. More care was given to the identification and interment of Union dead, and they were buried individually or in small groups. The Confederate dead were buried in large burial trenches dug in spots where the fighting was heaviest. This was quicker and more efficient, considering the weather.

In the late 1860s, the Federal government removed as many Union dead as possible to Shiloh National Cemetery. The wounds of battle were still fresh enough in the minds of those in charge of this effort to deny Confederates the

While Shiloh National Cemetery presents an orderly arrangement of graves today, in the aftermath of battle, the scope of the carnage was such that no one knew what to make of the horror and chaos. (cm)

same treatment, and so their remains were left in the large burial trenches that mark the landscape at Shiloh. At least 12 such trenches are known to exist on the battlefield grounds, but only five are marked.

It was grisly work to bury a number of men in a trench. Federal General Order Number 33 specified exactly how burial trenches were to be constructed: burial details were to pull the dead into a row, then begin the interment process by digging a long hole against the first man in line. Once he was laid in the hole, the ground was dug up where he had previously lain. This provided soil to cover the first body while simultaneously digging a hole for the second.

Theoretically, this assured an orderly burial of remains. In practice, burials were much less standard. Often natural depressions in the ground were used to begin a burial pit, and bodies were piled into these makeshift trenches. Severely decomposed corpses were pulled from the battlefield rather unceremoniously, using a system of metal hooks and stretchers intended to keep the remains as intact as possible and to avoid physically handling them.

Private Lucius W. Barber, Company D, 15th Illinois,

Veatch's Brigade, wrote in his memoirs, "Now we turned our attention to the rebel dead. We noticed that the faces of all of them had turned black. On examination, we found that their canteens contained whisky and gunpowder which was, no doubt, the cause of it. It seems that this had been given to them just before going into battle to make them fight. . . . It took two days to bury all of them."

Author Ambrose Bierce was merely Pvt. Ambrose Bierce when he walked the battlefield, searching for bodies. In the caustic manner he would later become famous for, he described what he and his unit came upon:

Later in life, Ambrose Bierce's dark literary sensibilities remained forever haunted by his experiences at Shiloh. (loc)

> *Forbidding enough it was in every way. . . . Death had put his sickle into this thicket and fire had gleaned the field. Along a line . . . lay the bodies . . . some in the unlovely looseness of attitude denoting sudden death by the bullet, but by far the greater number in postures of agony that told of the tormenting flame. Some were swollen to double girth; others shriveled to manikins. . . . their faces were bloated and black or yellow and shrunken. The contraction of muscles which had given them claws for hands had cursed each countenance with a hideous grin. Faugh! I cannot catalogue the charms of these gallant gentlemen who had got what they enlisted for.*

*   *   *

One of the more interesting aspects of the aftermath of the battle of Shiloh involved a strange visual phenomenon observed at night. Many soldiers were forced to lie in the mud and muck for two days while waiting for the medics to get to them. When the sun went down, an eerie blue-green glow began to be seen in several areas of the darkened Tennessee battlefield. Strangely, the wounds of some of the stranded soldiers were emitting this glow. No one had any idea what this phenomenon might portend, but the doctors and nurses noticed that those whose wounds had glowed brightly in the dark had a significantly higher survival rate than those whose wounds were not illuminated. Additionally, the wounds healed at a faster rate, and more cleanly. Because of these seemingly magical properties, the coloration became known as "Angel's Glow."

In 2001, two high school students finally solved this 139-year-old mystery. Bill Martin and his family were visiting the Shiloh Battlefield Park. They heard the stories about the strange glow, and Martin asked his mother, a microbiologist at the USDA Agricultural Research Center, if this phenomenon might have something in common with the micro-luminescent bacteria she had studied. Martin and his friend, Jon Curtis, researched the luminescent bacterium *Photorhabdus luminescens*, which lives in the guts of parasitic nematodes, a type of invertebrate also known as roundworms. When nematodes vomit up the glowing bacteria, *P. luminescens* kills other microbes living in the nematode's host, which at Shiloh would have been the body of a soldier.

Martin and Curtis studied the historical records and nighttime conditions at Shiloh during the battle. Normally *P. luminescens* dies at human body temperature, but the students found that temperatures on the battlefield in 1862 were low enough for soldiers to develop hypothermia. This allowed the bioluminescent bacteria to live and multiply in the bodies of wounded soldiers, to kill off competing parasitic bacteria, and to help save the lives of their human hosts. The eerie "Angel Glow" surrounding the wounds of some soldiers at Shiloh—and later, Gettysburg—was the bioluminescence of *P. luminescens.*

For solving this mystery, Bill Martin and Jon Curtis received first place in the 2001 Intel International Science and Engineering Fair.

At Shiloh National Battlefield

In 1866, the War Department established a cemetery on the battlefield at Shiloh, in southwest Tennessee. It began as the "Pittsburg Landing National Cemetery" because it was planned to accommodate not only those who had fallen at the battle of Shiloh, but also those who had died in the myriad operations in the area. In the fall of 1866, workers disinterred bodies from 156 locations on the battlefield itself, and from 565 locations along the Tennessee River.

At first headstones were made of wood, but in 1876-77 these were replaced by granite stones. Now, tall stones mark the 3,584 identified remains, and shorter, square stones denote the 2,359 unknowns. In 1889, the name of the cemetery was changed to Shiloh National Cemetery. A superintendent cared for the cemetery until it was officially made part of Shiloh National Military Park in 1943.

The Shiloh Battlefield Visitor Center sits adjacent to the national cemetery. (cm)

Shiloh National Cemetery was established as a Civil War cemetery, but burials continued in the old cemetery up until 1984. In the newest section of the grounds, there are many veterans from World Wars I and II, Korea,

Three known Confederates are buried in the national cemetery. Their stones have pointed rather than rounded tops. (cm)

Vietnam, and the Persian Gulf. There are still a few burials a year, mostly of widows of soldiers already interred.

Of the known soldiers, several interesting graves should be mentioned. Near the river are the remains of six color bearers from Wisconsin, all of whom died carrying their unit's standards into battle. To the west of these graves lie Capt. Edward Saxe of the 16th Wisconsin and John D. Holmes of the 15th Iowa. Saxe was the first Federal officer to fall at Shiloh, and 15-year-old Holmes was a young drummer boy.

Sadly, interspersed between all the identified American soldiers are countless gravestones with only a number identifying them. These men, too, served America. They had lives, mothers, perhaps wives, sons, and daughters, fears, hopes, and dreams, and their graves deserve as much honor as any other resting place.

There are three tombstones with pointed tops rather than the rounded ones of the U.S. soldiers—these are the burial sites of the only Confederates buried in Shiloh National Cemetery. These men died while being held as prisoners of war within Union lines. Heated debates were sparked by the fact that, other than these three, no Confederates are buried at Shiloh. Federal cemetery regulations, however, allow only members of the United States Armed Forces to be buried in national cemeteries. As Confederates were not technically members of the U.S. military, they have traditionally been buried elsewhere. In many cases, post-bellum groups of women and veterans created their own cemeteries for the Confederate dead, and many still feel that is the way things should remain.

The thousands of Confederates who died at Shiloh on those bleak days of early April were not removed from their original battlefield graves. They remain on the battlefield in at least 12 mass graves and in several individual plots. The park commission has only been able to locate and identify five of these burial sites. These are now marked, and the largest of them can be seen at the park's Tour Stop #5.

The National Cemetery is at the upper eastern corner of the Battlefield Park, and can be accessed easily. If you are planning to visit the cemetery and battlefield, check ahead to find out any costs or restrictions that may be affecting the area during your visit at www.nps.gov/shil/index.htm.

In 1911, beautiful ornamental iron gates were added to the cemetery. (cm)

At the Ambrose Bierce House BDB

For those readers who live in California, or who are planning to visit California's northern wine country, think about staying at the Ambrose Bierce house in St. Helena, California. Mr. Bierce actually owned and lived in the house, which was built in 1872. There are four guestrooms named for famous Californians like Eadweard Muybridge and Lily Langtry, and each is decorated with soft yellow and peach, antiques, and lace curtains. There is a crystal decanter of local port in each suite, and the bookshelves are filled with interesting reading, including many examples of work written by Bierce.

There is a champagne (again, local) breakfast served daily, with a wide choice of specialties like eggs Benedict and stuffed French toast. The coffee is especially good—hot and strong. In the later part of the afternoon, local artisanal cheeses and baked goods are offered as a small repast, accompanied by a selection of local wines. There are Spa packages and Wine Tour packages, as well as summer discounts.

The Bierce house is located at 1515 Main Street, in St. Helena, California. The website is www.ambrosebiercehouse.com. (mg)

FOR GOD AND COUNTRY – FOUNDED 1919

ORIGIN OF TAPS

AMERICAN WAR DEAD OF ALL WARS

Fading Light Dims the Sight

CHAPTER THREE

JULY 2, 1862

Cooler evening breezes stirred the leaves of the little peach trees in the orchard around Harrison's Landing. The brick house of Berkeley Plantation looked inviting, but only officers got to sleep there. Soldiers got to sleep in dog tents on the ground.

July 2, 1862, seemed calm, especially after the cacophony of the last seven days of fighting. The boys all camped together that night: Jerome Case and Teddy DeClair, the two youngest to enlist at Plymouth, Michigan in 1861, Johnny Dowger and the brothers, August and Ferdinand Grubner, also from Plymouth. In fact, all the boys were from Plymouth, even the "old man," Joe Foster—at thirty-five, the oldest of the group.

Not everyone was here, however. Twenty-year old Josiah Cronkite had been killed by artillery on the twenty-seventh of June. Captain James DeFoe had promised he would write to Josiah's mother, but he had not had time yet. Saddest of all was Robert Brown. Just twenty-five, he had talked his cousin, Gehiel, into enlisting with him. It had seemed like a great idea then, back in '61—all the bands playing, flags flying, pretty girls out to wish them well. But Gehiel had been shot dead in the ranks the day before, and Bob was inconsolable. How was he going to tell them back home that he had lost Gehiel? There was simply no way.

The sun dipped low and finally disappeared. Summer days seemed so long, with the fighting and the dying, and finally the resting. The Plymouth men were

A monument commemorating the origin of "Taps" (opposite) stands in its own shrine on the banks of the James River on Berkeley Plantation. A memorial bench (above) added for the 150th anniversary pays tribute to composer Dan Butterfield on one side and bugler Oliver Norton on the other. (cm)(cm)

The 1st Massachusetts Artillery, stationed near Harrison's Landing, holds a funeral service for a fallen comrade. (loc)

quiet, thinking of the missing from their little number. Joe Foster dug around in his briar pipe, looking for a few shreds of tobacco to smoke before he slept. The Grubner brothers whispered promises to keep each other safe, and Teddy DeClair just lay quietly, still in shock at what he had been through and amazed he had survived. Each man in the little encampment turned their thoughts toward the two who were not with them that night and waited for the familiar martial bugle call to reminded them "lights out."

When it came, it was not familiar at all. Instead, bugler Oliver Norton blew twenty-four different notes—notes that somehow captured exactly the feeling of the camp that night. They were slow, mournful, yet somehow comforting, and they came to be known around the world as "Taps."

*   *   *

There is no bugle call better known today than "Taps," yet few realize its origin was in the American Civil War. By the time its first three notes are played, however, the bugle call is instantly recognizable. Its purpose is to tell the soldier, whether he or she is a student at a military school or a member of the armed services overseas and possibly in harm's way, that, for that evening, all is well. The guards are posted, and the garrison is secure. It is also instantly recognizable at military funerals.

One of the oft-told origin stories concerning "Taps" is that of Union Army Capt. Robert Ellicombe, who was with his men near Harrison's Landing in Virginia, 1862. The Confederate Army was camped nearby, and during the night Ellicombe heard a strangled cry for water from a terribly injured young man still lying on the battlefield. The captain decided to risk his life to bring the wounded man back to camp for medical attention. He crawled out to the battlefield on his stomach to reach the soldier and

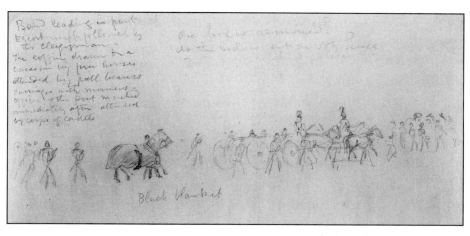

began pulling him back toward the Union encampment. When the captain reached his own lines, he discovered the man was actually a Confederate soldier, but had already died. The captain decided to risk lighting a lantern to see if he could learn more about the identification of the soldier. By the dim light, he gasped in shock when he realized the man was his own son. When Captain Ellicombe searched his son's knapsack for further information, he came upon a dirty, wadded-up piece of paper with some penciled notes inscribed upon it.

The following morning, heartbroken, the father asked permission of his superiors to give his son a full military burial despite his enemy status. His request was partially granted. There was no time for full military honors, so the captain requested a group of Army band members to play a funeral dirge at the funeral. That request was turned down, as well. However, out of respect for the father, he was allowed to have one musician. The captain chose a bugler. He asked the bugler to play the series of musical notes he found on the piece of paper in the dead youth's knapsack. These notes were the ones for "Taps."

Unfortunately, this poignant story comes to us from the television show *Ripley's "Believe It or Not."* On May 27, 1949 Robert Ripley's television show presented a short reenactment of this story, and many did, indeed "believe." Alas, the tale is absolutely fabricated. The truth, as is usually the case, is much more interesting.

Brigadier General Daniel A. Butterfield was commander of the Fifth Corps, 1st Division, 3rd Brigade of the Union Army under Maj. Gen. George C. McClellan. Butterfield loved martial music, and was especially fond of bugle calls. Bugle calls were very important during the Civil War. They were often the only way a group of men knew what to do next, as the piercing notes of the bugle could usually be heard

As a band leads the procession and the clergyman follows, a caisson bears a coffin toward burial while mourners walk behind. (loc)

Brig. Gen. Daniel Butterfield not only wrote "Taps" during the Peninsula Campaign, he also won the Medal of Honor for actions there during the battle of Gaines Mill on June 17, 1862. According to his citation, he "Seized the colors of the 83d Pennsylvania Volunteers at a critical moment and, under a galling fire of the enemy, encouraged the depleted ranks to renewed exertion." (loc)

over the din of battle. Butterfield noticed quickly that, although soldiers in a fight could hear the bugle, they were not certain if the call was directed at them or at another regiment. Butterfield's solution to this dilemma was to write his own bugle calls. His men learned to recognize these calls from the others and were better able to follow the bugled instructions.

Prior to the creation of "Taps," both the Union and Confederate armies used a French call named "Lights Out." According to bugler and brass historian Jari Villanueva, Butterfield felt this call was too martial and not reflective enough of the pride he felt for his brigade. He wanted to compose something special for his men, so he took the last five-and-a half measures of an earlier bugle call that had gone out of service and rearranged them. He fooled around with it some, then called in his brigade bugler Oliver W. Norton, known as O. W. to his family and friends. Together they worked out the details, and on the evening of July 2, 1862, on the grounds of the Berkeley Plantation, Norton blew "Taps" for the first time.

By the next morning, Norton was beseiged by other buglers who wanted to know more about his new call. He played it for them, shared the notes, and in a matter of days, "Taps" was being used by the entire Army of the Potomac. It spread to the rest of the Union Army, and from there the Confederates picked it up, as well.

The name "Taps" came from the Dutch word *taptoe*. As early as the 1500s, a group of musicians would march through a village of an evening, beating on a drum. This was the signal for bartenders to turn off the beer taps and for all soldiers to return to camp for the final roll call of the day. "Taps" also refers to the three drum taps that a drummer plays on the parade ground to signal lights out if there is no bugler available. It was shortened from "drum taps" to simply "taps," and this was the name that Civil War soldiers gave to Butterfield's composition.

Captain John C. Tidball started the custom of playing "Taps" at a military funeral. In early July 1862, at Harrison's Landing, a corporal of Tidball's Battery A, 2nd Artillery, died from wounds sustained in the Seven Days battles. "He was," Tidball recalled later, "a most excellent man." Tidball wanted to bury him with full military honors, but was refused. It was thought that the firing of the traditional three shots over the artilleryman's grave would give away the Federal position. Tidball later wrote, "The thought suggested itself to me to sound 'Taps' instead, which I did. The idea was taken up by others, until in a short time it was adopted by the entire army and is now looked upon as the most appropriate and touching part of a military funeral."

As Tidball proudly proclaimed, "Battery A has the

honor of having introduced this custom into the service, and it is worthy of historical note." Ten months later, "Taps" was played at the funeral of Confederate general Stonewall Jackson. By 1891, Army infantry regulations required "Taps" to be played at military funerals.

"Taps" was heard worldwide on television at the funeral of U. S. President John F. Kennedy. This was the first time an entire nation had witnessed a military funeral at Arlington and heard the song now used as "the final piece of music" when a veteran is laid to rest.

But for Civil War soldiers like Teddy DeClair, Robert Brown, and the Grubner brothers, those twenty-four notes meant a safe night, perhaps their last.

At Berkeley Plantation

Berkeley Plantation can boast of being not only the birthplace of "Taps" but also of the first official Thanksgiving, observed in 1619. It's also the ancestral home of the Harrison family. Benjamin Harrison, a signer of the Declaration of Independence and governor of Virginia, and President William Henry "Tippecanoe" Harrison were both born there, and President Benjamin Harrison traced his roots there.

Guides in colonial-era costume conduct daily tours of the house. Self-guided tours of the grounds invite visitors to explore beautiful gardens, the family cemetery, monuments to Taps and the first Thanksgiving, and a stunning overlook of the James River.

For more information on this historical landmark, visit their website: www.berkeleyplantation.com.

Boxwoods line the front walkway to the main house, which dates back to 1726. (cm)

| "Taps" (in the written key of C) | Day is done, gone the sun, from the lakes from the hills from the sky, all is well, safely, rest, God is near. | Fading light, Dims the sight, And a star gems the sky Gleaming bright, From afar, Drawing, near, Falls the night. | Thanks and praise, For our days, Neath the sun Neath the stars Neath the sky, As we go, This, we, know, God is near. |

ℬodies ℒaid in 𝒪ur 𝒟ooryards

CHAPTER FOUR

SEPTEMBER 17, 1862

The Pry House Field Hospital Museum, sponsored by the National Museum of Civil War Medicine, opened in 2005. The Pry house, on the historic Philip Pry farm, served as Union Gen. George McClellan's headquarters during the battle of Antietam. President Abraham Lincoln visited it two weeks after the battle. Exhibits in the house and barn include the recreation of a wartime operating theater, interpretive panels and artifacts relating to the care of wounded soldiers, an exhibit showcasing the effects on the civilian population of the battle and its aftermath, and more information on the Pry house itself. Contact the websites listed below for the suggested entrance donation, and to confirm the hours of operation for the Pry house: www.nps.gov/anti/planyourvisit/pryhouse.htm or www.civilwarmed.org/pry-house-field-hospital-museum/visit-the-pry-house/ (cm)

Alexander Gardner shook his head as he looked around for the best place to start. He was at Antietam Creek, in Sharpsburg, Maryland, on September 19 to photograph the battlefield two days after the battle of Antietam. The job was not going to be easy, although the main photographic problem—that of the movement of the subjects—was a non-issue. Dead men don't move.

Gardner's employer, photographer Mathew Brady, had asked for at least 70 collodion plates to be made as quickly as possible—quickly, because in the heat and humidity of mid-September in southern Maryland, a corpse could *go bad* very fast.

The battle of Antietam, known in the South as the battle of Sharpsburg, was fought on September 17, 1862. Part of the Maryland campaign, it was the first major battle of the Civil War to occur on Union soil. It is also the bloodiest single-day battle in American history, with a combined count of 22,717 dead, wounded, and missing. Union Maj. Gen. George McClellan pursued and attacked Confederate Gen. Robert E. Lee's Army of Northern Virginia, winning a narrow victory for the North.

Gardner's assistant, James F. Gibson, pointed out a probable location for an image, and the two men got to work. They moved across the battlefield, past the Dunker Church, through the Cornfield, across Burnside's Bridge, down Bloody Lane, then back again. Union and Confederate dead filled the glass plates trundled along in the Whatsit Wagon, carefully driven by Alfred Foons, who had to dodge the burial details at their grisly work.

It was a good day's work, but pretty bad as well. The stench was unbelievable, and it would get worse if there were any further delay. Sam Fletcher of the 15th Massachusetts wrote about his experience as part of a

Alexander Gardner (left) working for Matthew Brady (right) essentially invented the practice of photojournalism through their work with _The Dead of Antietam_. Gardner did some brilliant photography in the field, but because he worked for Brady, Brady often got the credit. This eventually led to a split between the men. (mg)(loc)

burial detail on September 18: "It was hot and the bodies were getting soft and it was very unpleasant. . . . I tasted the odor for several days."

Weather showed little respect for the fallen. It had rained on both the living and the dead after the battle at Manassas and in between the two days of Shiloh. Now the sun was beating down on just under 4,000 dead soldiers. This number was, and still is, simply astounding. More Americans died on this battlefield than had died, or would ever die, on any one day in the nation's military history.

Soldiers such as Charles A. Hale of the 5th New Hampshire wrote to his wife on September 19, telling her, "What a bloody place was that sunken road as we advanced and the Irish Brigade fell back; the fences went down on both sides, and the dead and wounded men were literally piled there in heaps."

Gardner and Gibson moved from such ghastly groupings to individual men, memorializing the carnage of battle. They worked quickly, ducking under the hood behind the still camera, counting off seconds, then rushing the plate, still in its frame, back to the darkness of the little Whatsit Wagon for safekeeping.

Over two days, Gardner and Gibson took more than 90 images, then they drove back to Washington, D.C.

*   *   *

Mathew Brady's studio was usually a quiet place where politicians and generals came to have their portraits made for posterity, but as soon as Gardner and Gibson returned, it became a bustling mixture of pyrogallic acid and sodium thiosulfate as the plates were processed and varnished for their trip north.

Brady's first studio, on Broadway in New York, had opened in 1844. Brady's reputation had grown greatly since that time, based for the most part on images of the famous and soon-to-be-famous. In 1849, Brady opened

a smaller studio in Washington, making it easier to continue to photograph the politicians and fire-eaters. By 1861, he was positive that creating a photographic documentation of the coming war was his mission. "I had to go," he said just before that first battle at Manassas. "A spirit in my feet said 'Go,' and I went."

Brady's eyesight had begun to deteriorate, though, so he hired a group of talented photographers, including Gardner and Gibson, to travel to the battlefields and photograph the war. After obtaining permission from President Abraham Lincoln, Brady sent his teams into every place possible, bringing back over 10,000 images during the course of the conflict.

Brady had described himself as a "historian with a camera."

* * *

On the evening of October 20, 1862, Mathew Brady turned the small sign around on the door of his New York studio. It read, "The Dead of Antietam."

On the studio walls hung a series of 90 painfully explicit visual images, giving the citizens of New York City their first views of the unbelievable bloody fighting around Antietam Creek. For most New Yorkers, these were also their first views of any sort of battlefield deaths. Newspapers at the time could not yet reproduce

The dead Confederates sprawled in the field across from Dunker Church (top) may have been artillerists in Parker's Battery, or they may have been infantrymen killed in a desperate counterattack against Federals who had penetrated as far as the church. Today, a historical marker explains the scene (bottom). (loc)(cm)

photographs. Instead, they ran elaborate woodcuts made to recreate the images of the camera. In the 1860s, there were also daguerreotypes and *cartes de visite* (CDVs) in many American households. A stereopticon viewer was a staple on many parlor tables, along with cards bearing double images of Niagara Falls or parts of the Erie Canal.

None of these images, however, were of badly maimed, decomposing corpses.

What made Brady's photographic exhibit so important to the way Americans in 1862 saw the history through which they were living? Why does it still resonate with us today, as a *memento mori* of the aftermath of war?

By 1865, the citizens of New York had delivered more than 360,000 men to the battlefields of the Civil War. Yet because the fighting was geographically far away, they could distance themselves from the intensity of the action on a daily basis. The confused mass of names in their morning papers were, probably, just names of strangers, easy to forget when the breakfast coffee was finished. It was difficult to connect any of those names with the bloody, mangled, decomposing corpse of someone's son, brother, father, sweetheart, or husband—difficult and unpleasant.

But suddenly Mathew Brady, imminent photographer of the rich and famous, decided to fill the walls of his studio with just such images. In the words of an October 20, 1862, *New York Times* editorial writer, "If he had not brought bodies and laid them in our dooryards and along the streets, he has done something very like it." The dead of Antietam had become very much alive to the men and women who climbed the stairs to the small gallery to peer, sometimes with a magnifying glass in hand, at the barely distinguishable features of soldier corpses.

The "strange spell that dwells in dead men's eyes" drew crowds for weeks to Brady's rooms. Hushed groups of living people crowded around images of dead ones, and saw, many for the first time, what death looked like when it happened suddenly and violently, far away from the caring hands of home. The weak October sun that fell upon New Yorkers was the same sun that had earlier blackened the swollen faces of the slain, blistering them

and hastening corruption. And not just men, but horses and mules, piles of each, stacked like wood ready for winter fireplaces.

It was too much for some, who fainted, and others, who anxiously perused Brady's photographs looking for the familiar face of someone they loved. But it was just enough for Mathew Brady. His idea of making the war real, present, and true had been a good one. Reactions were gratifying. Brady had no idea he would be known as the father of photojournalism; he just knew that customers who looked at the images taken by his photographers were not the same people when they descended the stairs as they had been before they went up. They had seen for themselves just how horrible the war was, and there were no words to convey the ugly reality quite as well as these images had.

When we look at these photographs over 150 years later, time suddenly collapses. Exactly what these images show is truly the aftermath of battle. Most of the pictures were taken at medium distances from the subject, and many were photographed from a variety of angles. This enables the viewer to see not only the subject itself, but the scope of the destruction surrounding the dead: the ground torn up by shot and shell, the crushed grass matted down with blood, the messy piles of clothing and accouterments left behind.

Some of the images seem to have been staged, and indeed they were. Today this staging would be considered unethical, but photography was in its infancy, and a picture was there to illustrate a larger story. It was not yet an artifact of history in its own right. One image shows the unburied body of a Confederate soldier lying

As works of journalism, *The Dead of Antietam* had a huge impact because of their immediacy—the equivalent, in their day, of Edward R. Murrow broadcasting from London rooftops during the Battle of Britain or Walter Cronkite broadcasting from the jungles of Vietnam. (loc)

next to the burial mound of a Union soldier. It was a Union victory, after all. The Confederates were not there to bury their dead. Some corpses have their swollen faces turned in the direction of the camera. The photographer or an assistant posed some in this manner, on purpose, so that those doing the viewing could *see* the dead, see the men who had "not hesitated to seal and stamp their convictions with their blood."

It is the photographs of Mathew Brady's teams of brilliant photographers—Alexander Gardner, Timothy O'Sullivan, William Pywell, James Gibson, George Barnard, Thomas Roche, and 17 others, acting like a small newspaper operation—that still give us our images of the Civil War. The work of Brady's photographers changed the way his contemporaries saw war. It was experience with Brady's organization that gave many of these artists the opportunity to establish themselves as photographers in their own right. Their work has continued to enable us to view battlefields, camps, towns, cities, and people touched by war for over 150 years. No student of the Civil War goes untouched by these images. With the process of digitalization, they become even more important to our understanding of the conflict, from its whole and handsome young soldiers to the heart-wrenchingly sad and haunting aftermath of battle.

At Antietam National Battlefield

"Old Simon" stands vigil over the dead of Antietam at the national cemetery. (dw)

After September 17, 1862, the small town of Sharpsburg, Maryland, turned into a hospital and burial ground, with private houses as well as government-sponsored hospital tents extending miles in every direction. In 1864, Maryland State Senator

Lewis P. Firey introduced to the senate a bill to establish some sort of funded cemetery in which to bury the men who died in the Maryland campaign of 1862. On March 23, 1865, Maryland established a burial site with the purchase of 11.25 acres adjoining Sharpsburg for $1,161.75. Originally the burial ground was to have held the remains of Union and Confederate dead, but the inability of the South to pay a fair share of the cost coupled with the ill feelings of losing the war caused Maryland to withdraw her offer. Only Union dead are interred at Antietam Cemetery. Confederate remains were buried at several surrounding cemeteries, and over 60% of the 2,800 men who fought for the South remain unidentified.

One of the most striking monuments of the area is the Private Soldier Monument. It was initially exhibited at the Philadelphia Centennial Exposition, in 1876. On September 17, 1880, 16 years after the battle, it finally was unveiled and formally dedicated at the Antietam Cemetery. Known lovingly as "Old Simon," the monument is inscribed, "Not for themselves, but for their country."

Of special interest is December's Annual Antietam National Battlefield Memorial Illumination. Traditionally held on the first Saturday in December, it features 23,000 candles—one each for every soldier killed, wounded, or missing at the battle of Antietam.

The Antietam Cemetery is south of the Antietam Visitor Center, down Highway 65 and left on Highway 34 (the Boonsboro Pike). It is just northwest of Burnside Bridge.

Visit   www.nps.gov/anti/historyculture/antietam-national-cemetery.htm

The Antietam battleground is in especially beautiful condition thanks to the National Park Service. The Visitor Center is at 5831 Dunker Church Road, in Sharpsburg, Maryland. There are many ways to view the battlefield, and the signage is excellent. The park's website offers suggestions for tours based on the amount of time a visitor has to spend at the battlefield. Park rangers give regular tours, and self-guided tours are available, as are self-guided hikes. Summer weekends offer demonstrations of artillery and weapons firing on the battlefield itself. For more information about this and other programs, including Independence Day, Memorial Day, the anniversary of the battle of Antietam, and special programs for children and teachers, visit the website: www.nps.gov/anti/planyourvisit/index.htm. (cm)

A Singleness of Spirit

CHAPTER FIVE

There is a particularly famous photograph of a dead horse taken at Antietam after the battle. This iconic image has affected nearly everyone who has ever seen it. Union Gen. Alpheus S. Williams, in his own Civil War memoirs, wrote about the scene:

> *The number of dead horses was high. They lay, like the men, in all attitudes. One beautiful milk-white animal had died in so graceful a position that I wished for its photograph. Its legs were doubled under and its arched neck gracefully turned to one side, as if looking back to the ball-hole in its side. Until you got to it, it was hard to believe the horse was dead.*

More than 1.5 million horses and mules were killed during the Civil War. In earlier accounts, the number is closer to one million, but just as the human death toll for the war has risen due to revised counting, so have the non-human numbers increased. At Gettysburg alone between 3,000 and 5,000 horses and mules were killed. For every soldier killed in the Civil War, almost five horses died as well. Union Maj. Gen. John Gibbon, in observation of the horses in Lt. Alonzo Cushing's 4th U.S. Artillery at Gettysburg, wrote:

> *One thing which forcibly occurred to me was the perfect quiet with which the horses stood in their places. Even when a shell, striking in the midst of a team, would knock over one or two of them or hurl one struggling in its death agonies to the ground, the rest would make no effort to struggle or escape but would stand stolidly by as if saying to themselves, "It is fate, it is useless to try to avoid it."*

It is impossible to imagine the Civil War without horses. When the war broke out in the spring of 1861,

The Civil War Horses and Mules Memorial, a three-quarter-size bronze, was installed in the courtyard of the National Sporting Library in Middleburg, Virginia, in 1999. (cm)

Photographed by Alexander Gardner, this horse looks as though it laid down for a peaceful nap. However, it was one of *The Dead of Antietam.* (loc)

there were approximately 3.4 million horses in the Northern states, 1.7 million in the Confederate states, and about 800,000 in the border states of Missouri and Kentucky. There were fewer horses in the South because a blooded horse was a sign of elite power. Horses were a leisure-oriented purchase. For the most part, they were bred, driven, and ridden for speed and pleasure. Southern bloodstock included Thoroughbreds, American Standardbreds, Morgans, and Tennessee Walkers.

Northern horses were bred to work. They were bigger and rougher, many times bred from draught horses. They pulled plows and other machinery in the country and wagons and public conveyances in the city. Only the wealthy could afford such luxuries as a matched pair of carriage horses or a mount for personal pleasure riding.

When the war began, West Point-educated, upper class officers led the Confederate military, complete with blooded horses from their own stables. Throughout the war, the Confederate cavalry was renowned for its horses as well as for its skill while riding them. A cavalryman had to provide his own horse—which led to a chronic shortage of both men and mounts.

In the summer of 1863, the Confederate Army of Northern Virginia confiscated horses and mules from Pennsylvania to replace those lost to the rigors of war. A good warhorse—cavalry, artillery, or wagon train—had to be trained to not react badly to guns and cannon. Pennsylvania's horses and mules took a while to learn their new trade.

Lack of military experience was an issue for both horses and men in the North. The U.S. Army traditionally used horses as transportation, not in combat. The cavalry was not considered a fighting arm of the service, but rather a quick way to send messages between commanders. By 1863, however, the Union cavalry was coming into its own. New ideas concerning the purpose of a mounted arm, better training, as well as the intelligent purchasing of many Morgan and Standardbred horses by the Quartermaster Department finally gave

the Federals an equal footing with the Confederates on the battlefield. In June, the Union made a strong showing against J. E. B. Stuart's troopers in the battle of Brandy Station. After the battle of Gettysburg in July, even with all the loss of life—human and equine—the Union cavalry fought on. They pursued Lee's army, capturing or destroying more than half of Stuart's men and reclaiming 4,000 horses and mules, and 1,000 wagons loaded with food and fodder.

Because of their size and weight, horse carcassss proved difficult to move. Many were often burned where they fell, but those that lay too close to a tree or building could not be set afire and had to be left to rot. (loc)

When fighting was especially horrific or retreats became disorderly, an officer mounted on a handsome horse could often encourage his men or turn a rout into a charge. One famous example is that of Union Maj. Gen. Phil Sheridan and his big, black war horse Rienzi. Sheridan often said his mount was

> *an animal of great intelligence and immense strength and endurance. He always held his head high, and by the quickness of his movements gave many persons the idea that he was exceedingly impetuous. This was not so, for I could at any time control him by a firm hand and a few words, and he was as cool and quiet under fire as one of my soldiers. I doubt if his superior as a horse for field service was ever ridden by any one.*

Rienzi and Sheridan were together for the last three years of the war, through 45 engagements, two cavalry raids, and 19 pitched battles. The horse was wounded many times, but recovered. Sheridan rode his reliable charger at Appomattox, when Robert E. Lee surrendered the Army of the Potomac to Ulysses S. Grant.

For every Rienzi, though, hundreds of horses and mules perished. Horses frequently took bullets for their riders, especially if their riders were officers. Confederate

Artillery and cavalry units were particularly dependent on horses, but the entire army relied on them. The loss of horses and mules affected transportation, communication, and intelligence-gathering capabilities—not to mention its combat effectiveness. (loc)

Gen. Joseph Orville Shelby had 24 horses shot out from under him. Confederate cavalry commander Nathan Bedford Forrest lost 39 mounts. General George Custer holds the highest Union toll for horse-loss at 11.

Losing equines one at a time was bad enough; losing them in larger groups was terrible. The artillery relied on horses to move heavy cannons from place to place. The men who served the guns rode on the caissons or with the limber chests, not horses. Artillery horses were commonly big mules or draft horses. John Gibbon, quoted above, also commented on desirable traits for an artillery horse:

> *The horse for artillery service should be from fifteen to sixteen hands high and should stand erect on his legs, be strongly built, but free in his movements; his shoulders should be large enough to give support to the collar but not too heavy; his body full, but not too long; the sides well rounded; the limbs solid with rather strong shanks, and the feet in good condition. To these qualities he should unite, as much as possible, the qualities of the saddle horse; should trot and gallop easily, have even gaits and not be skittish.*

Seeing images of the dead is a powerful experience, but one might argue that each man made a decision to be where he was. This is not the case for the animals that lost their lives. They were merely the expendable servants of a cause. Yet they died, just as surely as the men who cared for them and depended on them, and burying a horse is not an easy task. The method established by both armies was to pile up the dead horses and mules and set fire to the remains. The stench of burning, rotten horsemeat rose high on the greasy, dark smoke—a funeral pyre of incredible proportions. The only duty worse for a soldier than burying humans was dealing with animals in the aftermath of battle.

If not already dead, the animals were hysterical with pain and confusion, and for those reasons, apt to be dangerous. The seriously wounded were shot. There was little veterinary care for them anyway. Then their bodies were dragged into piles and set on fire. It was sad work all around—and never-ending. A battlefield was not *clean* until the equine carcasses were removed, along with the human remains.

A fitting tribute to the importance of horses in the war came at Appomattox, on April 9, 1865. Confederate terms of surrender were not unconditional, as Grant's one-time nickname, "Unconditional Surrender," might suggest. Although Lee agreed that his men would give up their guns, both he and Grant were in complete agreement that the Confederate soldiers would be able to keep their horses, if they had one. Many once-fiery war steeds turned their heads away from the battlefields and started home. Plows needed to be pulled and crops put in, now that the war was over.

> There is
> Some indescribable communion
> Between a man and a horse
> Who've shared the roughest roads,
> The longest hours,
> The hardest battles;
> A singleness of spirit, faith unflagging.
>
> —from "The General's Mount" by Jack Knox

A number of specific Civil War horses have their own memorials: Robert E. Lee's Traveller (below) and Stonewall Jackson's Little Sorrel are both in Lexington, Virginia; Phil Sheridan's Rienzi is in the Smithsonian's Museum of American History; George Meade's Old Baldy is in the Grand Army of the Republic Museum in Philadelphia. In Tipp City, Ohio (above), a monument stands to the horse of Civil War veteran Daniel Rouzer. (mmc)

Real War Horses

Memorials to dead horses and mules are difficult to find. One way to go about it is to look for the inclusion of animals in cemetery statuary, such as Sallie, the Staffordshire bull terrier mascot of the 11th Pennsylvania Infantry. She still guards her "boys" at the base of the 11th PA monument at Gettysburg.

Any mounted depiction of Robert E. Lee will show him on his warhorse, Traveller, probably the best known of all the general's horses. Lee rode other horses—Richmond, The Roan, Lucy Long, and Ajax—but he preferred the grey Morgan with the black mane and tail above all others. Traveller is buried on the campus of Washington and Lee University in Lexington, Virginia, outside of Lee Chapel, where his owner is entombed.

Aside from Traveller, three other Civil War horses have been honored individually: Sheridan's Rienzi,

Robert E. Lee's horse, Traveller, is buried outside Lee's crypt. (cm)

For more information about the three versions of the Civil War Horse and Mule Memorial, check the appropriate websites for public accessibility of these monuments. (cm)(cm)

TOP: The Virginia Historical Society in Richmond, Virginia: www.vahistorical.org

BOTTOM: National Sporting Library and Museum in Middleburg, Virginia: www.nsl.org

NOT PICTURED: U. S. Cavalry Museum at Fort Riley, Kansas: www.riley.army.mil/AboutUs/Museums.aspx

Confederate Lt. Gen. "Stonewall" Jackson's Little Sorrel, and Union Maj. Gen. George Gordon Mead's Old Baldy.

Three monuments honor the collective contributions of Civil War horses and mules. The original one is *The Civil War Horses and Mules Memorial*. It is a three-quarter-size bronze that resides in the courtyard of the National Sporting Library. A book published in 1993 and given to Paul Mellon, a millionaire horse-breeder and philanthropist, inspired the statue, which is dedicated to the equine blood shed in the Civil War. Mellon was adamant that the horse image used would reflect the deprivations and hard use endured by the horses and mules in the Civil War. He insisted that sculptor Tessa Pullan be authentic in every way, including showing the horse's ribs and having him stand with his back hoof bent, because "horses stand that way when they are tired."

The library's horse was completed in 1997, but Mr. Mellon was not finished. He commissioned an identical statue, *The Civil War Horse*, for the U.S. Cavalry Museum in Fort Riley, Kansas. He also wanted a third to be placed in the garden at Richmond's Virginia Historical Society. He decided the three-quarter-size horse was too small, so he had another mold made to full size for the third bronze. Mr. Mellon died in 1999, so Virginia's *The War Horse* is probably the last version of his original idea to be erected.

One other statue of a Civil War horse sits behind the post office in Tipp City, Ohio. It marks the resting place of Capt. Daniel M. Rouzer's horse, whose name is not known. Daniel Rouzer joined the Union Army in 1861, when he was 43, serving in the 8th Ohio Cavalry. He rode his horse home after the war in 1865. He valued the animal and claimed it had saved his life. When it died, he had it buried on his property near the intersection of West Main Street (State Route 571) and Fourth. A post office was built near the location, but great care was taken not to disturb the remains of Rouzer's horse.

Later on, there was some suspicion as to whether the horse was really buried there, but the land has been kept clear, just in case. Philip and Lois Cox, of the Philip G. Cox Insurance Company, now own the land, and are responsible for the statue of the unknown Civil War mount whose owner loved him. A visit to Tipp City might be delightful as well as historic. Their website is www.visittippcity.org.

*   *   *

The real truth, however, is much simpler than stuffed horses or bronze statues. Beneath the ground of almost every place that was occupied for any length of time by an army during the Civil War is a testament to the horses and mules that moved those armies. Their bones lie beneath the sod, perhaps burned to ash, perhaps scavenged by insect life, perhaps completely decayed by now. The remains of the mules from the ill-fated Mud March of Union General Burnside; the burned carcasses of the horses of Antietam, Shiloh, and Gettysburg; the equine corpses of animals shot by a Confederate army with no extra food to spare to feed them—their deaths hallow their resting places as surely as those of soldiers do. Animals do not decide to go to war; they simple obey to the best of their ability, trusting in the humans who give the orders. May they also rest in peace.

At Bentonville, North Carolina, a memorial to Civil War horses depicts a moving horse in artillery gear, with both C.S. and U.S. insignia on either side of the head. Privately commissioned by local resident Larry Laboda, sculptor Cary J. van Dansik of the Netherlands created the bronze memorial in November of 2011; Laboda installed it on a base created by Edgerton's Memorials in 2012. The horse, dubbed "Cannonball"--and another to the 123rd New York Infantry that Laboda also commissioned--are accessible by way of a gravel path in the front of Laboda's property, near the monument to Gen. Joseph Johnston. "I have no problem with visitors walking to see the sculpture," Laboda says. Nonetheless, visitors are urged to please be respectful of the property owner's privacy and property rights. (pg)

"Your Obedient Servant"

CHAPTER SIX

MAY 2, 1863

Private John Cady just lay there. About two hours had passed since he had received the wound in his upper thigh. It seemed quieter now in the little wooded area near Ely's Ford. It was getting dark and the shooting at a place called Chancellorsville seemed to have stopped. Calls for water and help had replaced the whirring buzz of the bullets.

He was afraid to move at all. What if moving made his leg worse? He'd seen other men wounded on the battlefield, and he'd seen the surgeries at the field hospitals. What a nightmare! It was better now, though. Back in '61, no one had any idea what to do with a wounded soldier. Now that Doc Letterman had joined up, there was a plan. The band didn't have to double as stretcher carriers. Ha! What a joke. Before the Doc, stretchers were just a blanket and a hope. Now there were proper stretchers, and men were trained to carry 'em. There were even ambulances that were 'specially designed not to knock a fellow's bones apart just getting him to the field tents. Gen'ral Hooker had finally allowed the Doc to move his medical wagons along with all the rest, so there were supposed to be supplies . . . gosh how his leg hurt. He ran his hand down toward his pants, feeling the wetness of the blood.

"John! John! That you? It's me—Dan. Dan Groves. Wave your hand if you hear me."

John waved his hand weakly. Dan had come, finally. Dan—who wore the green half-chevron of the Ambulance Corps, who had joined up with John in Dayton, Ohio, as members of the 1st Ohio Infantry, Company D, when Ol'

Jonathan Letterman's cross-shaped grave (above) sits atop a ridge at Arlington National Cemetery (opposite). (cm)(cm)

Fewer individuals in the Civil War made farther-reaching contributions than Dr. Jonathan Letterman. "I often wondered whether, had I been confronted with the primitive system which Letterman fell heir to at the beginning of the Civil War, I could have developed as good an organization as he did," said WWII's Maj. Gen. Paul Hawley, chief surgeon of the European Theater. "I doubt it. There was not a day during World War II that I did not thank god for Jonathan Letterman." (loc)

Abe had called for 75,000 in the first place.

Dan raced toward John, slid to a stop. *It's okay*, he said. *We've got you.*

* * *

Simple words—*It's okay. We've got you.*—but the men who served in the Army of the Potomac had waited until June 23, 1862, to hear them. Prior to that time, no one had given much thought to the needs of an army in the field, neither after a battle nor daily. In 1861, disease killed twice as many soldiers than battlefield injuries did. As much as 30 percent of the army's strength could be on sick call at any given time. Camp hygiene and the horrors of Civil War battlefields dealt the armies on both sides serious blows, and it was clear that both Union and Confederate military medical departments needed to reinvent themselves to cope with the thousands of wounded and dying men left in the aftermath of battle. Advances in weaponry had outpaced the army's medical department organization as well as its battle tactics, neither of which had changed in more than 50 years. Luckily for the Army of the Potomac, it had an officer with expertise, good sense, determination and unflagging energy: Dr. Jonathan Letterman.

Letterman, an army surgeon since 1849, when he graduated from Pennsylvania's Jefferson Medical College, was assigned to the Army of the Potomac in 1861. Previously he had served on a variety of military campaigns against Native American tribes in Florida, Minnesota, New Mexico, and California. He had never been in charge of the health care of more than a few hundred soldiers, and he had never done any surgery more difficult than the occasional removal of an arrowhead. Now the thin, quiet, thoughtful Letterman found himself charged with the medical responsibility of 50,000 men, many of whom were injured or ill.

Letterman was immediately dispatched to Harrison's Landing, as McClellan had chosen to retreat from the Peninsula and return to Washington. He was appalled by the conditions he found.

> *It was impossible to obtain proper reports of the number of sick in the army when it reached Harrison's Landing. After about six thousand had been sent away on the transports, twelve thousand seven hundred and ninety-five remained. . . . sickness amounted to at least twenty percent.*

In addition to being severely wounded, the men of the Army of the Potomac were lice-ridden, suffering from scurvy and chronic dysentery, malarial, riddled with typhus, chronic malnutrition, and raging infection in any open orifice, or any small cut or wound. Letterman found the entire situation completely unacceptable. He confronted Maj. Gen. George McClellan, and offered a plan that would become the first step in creating by an Act of Congress what became the standard medical procedure for the entire United States Army in 1864.

On July 8, 1862, McClellan issued Special Order No. 197, 139, and 150. Together, these three orders required an officer's approval for a soldier to be admitted to a hospital or to be evacuated; sanitary inspections, with reports sent to senior officers; and a regular supply of fresh vegetables to prevent scurvy. Bathing and human waste policies were established, and suggestions concerning proper food preparation became orders. "I think if these suggestions be carried into effect that we may with reason expect the health of this army to be in as good a state as that of any army in the field." By August, the Army of the Potomac disease rate declined by one third.

Letterman instituted battlefield triage procedures that brought wounded soldiers to designated spots for quicker treatments. (mg)

Military camp hygiene and an improvement in battlefield medical practices were priorities for Letterman. One of the ways he defined his job was to be able to provide his commanding general with as many healthy, active soldiers as possible. On a daily level, this meant healthier camp life, but it also meant that the army's medical department had to make some serious changes in how it conducted business. Outdated military tactics such as massing large numbers of men in front of lethal weaponry resulted in horrifically high casualty numbers. Nevertheless, caring for the wounded was often a secondary concern for most commanders. A general sought to win a battle, and was much more concerned with wagonloads of ammunition as opposed to wagonloads of medical supplies. Often the medical wagons were abandoned in the rush to battle. When the fighting ended, clearing the battlefield was often seen as a nuisance. This task was assigned to skulkers and whoever was willing to do the work. As soon as possible, the general in command removed his army from the battlefield, taking needed doctors, medical personnel, and supplies with him.

There were no corpsmen or medics. A wounded comrade was often escorted off the battlefield by that persistent handful of soldiers who simply had no stomach for fighting. These same soldiers often "got lost" on their way back to the action. Members of regimental bands were pressed into service, although there is no correlation between ferrying the wounded from the battlefield and playing a box valve cornet. Usually a soldier simply stayed where he fell, often remaining on the battlefield until his

calls for help were heard and he was dragged away. He could not be certain if his rescuers would be from his own army or the enemy. His survival depended on a painful, body-wrenching return to his own side and a makeshift first aid station in an old barn or under a tree, or an equally bone-jarring, brutal trip in a diseased and suffocating boxcar to a prisoner of war camp. Often, a man was simply left for days, to live or die. It was in God's hands, after all.

Letterman found all of this absolutely intolerable. He immediately set about to right these egregious wrongs. He created a comprehensive plan to handle the mass casualties of the battlefield, as well as synchronizing all the elements of their medical care afterward. The Letterman Plan is not one single document, but a series of reforms instituted over the year and a half he spent as Medical Director of the Army of the Potomac. "[I]t remained necessary to devise a system that would render as available as possible the material on the spot . . . and not wait for the arrival of such as had been asked for, only a portion of which ever came," wrote Letterman. His work was so forward in its thinking and implementation that parts of it are still in use in both military and civilian emergency medicine and disaster relief.

Stretcher bearers conducted drills (top) to more efficiently transport wounded soldiers and load them onto ambulances, which lined up in long trains (bottom), waiting for the incoming flood of wounded during battle. (loc)
(loc)

The Letterman Plan was a tiered system of treatment, taking care of issues in the order in which they were presented. A brief outline of the plan included

- creation of an organized Ambulance Corps
- regulations for organizing surgical field hospitals
- advent of forward first aid
- introduction of triage, including a three-tiered system of priority
- long-term recovery hospitals on the battlefield
- staged evacuation and treatment system

Prior to the implementation of General Order No. 147, there was no reliable system of evacuation for the wounded from the battlefield. Any conveyance was used, with no thought given to patient safety or comfort. Letterman personally designed safe conveyances detailed only for ambulance purposes. He created an Ambulance Corps of qualified and trained officers and corpsmen who wore a green band and green chevrons to differentiate them from combat soldiers.

Before the fall of 1862, there was no plan in place to care for the wounded who had been removed from the battlefield. Surgical Field Hospitals, staffed with skilled, qualified surgeons and other medical personnel were now affiliated with specific divisions. This simplified both medical care and record keeping for the army, but no one, not even the enemy, was ever turned away from any

facility. Forward First Aid combined with surgical field hospitals resulted in emergency care that began even before the fighting ended.

Early battlefield medicine operated on a first-come, first-served basis. The Letterman Plan introduced the idea of triage from European battlefields. Triage is a method by which a soldier's injuries are evaluated and treated in order of priority: First Priority—most serious but survivable wounds; Second Priority—less serious wounds; and Third Priority—likely fatal wounds. "Dressers" prepared soldiers for further treatment, and field surgeons finally received patients who had been cleaned up and stabilized. This greatly increased a soldier's chances of survival.

In the aftermath of a battle, Letterman's Plan provided for large tent hospitals to be constructed to house patients for up to several months. If a man was so severely wounded and unstable that he could not be evacuated by rail on special hospital cars or by water aboard hospital ships to large general hospitals in

When it came time for medical personnel to perform on the field, their drilling allowed them to carry out their jobs more effectively (top). A hospital wagon stands outside the Seminary Ridge Museum in Gettysburg (bottom). The Seminary was used as a hospital following the battle. (loc)(cm)

Letterman's system of care revolutionized army medicine. (loc)

major cities, he was cared for in a battlefield hospital. Military surgeons and corpsmen staffed these hospitals, although some of the burden of care still fell on the local community, which had borne all of it prior to the advent of field hospitals.

Letterman was not particularly concerned with the dead. As one Union surgeon wrote to his wife:

> *The days after the battle are a thousand times worse than the day of the battle—the physical pain is not the greatest pain suffered. . . . The dead appear sickening but they suffer no pain. But the poor wounded mutilated soldiers that yet have life and sensation make a most horrid picture.*

In less than four months, Jonathan Letterman had, almost single-handedly, eliminated the nightmare anarchy of removing the wounded from the battlefield. He organized a system of tiered hospital care, from stretchers and a first aid station to sustained medical care at a large general hospital many miles away. Letterman's organized, professional medical corps reliably procured the necessary supplies at each stage of the process. They established a measure of independence and control over their activities with a command structure and corpsmen dedicated to—ultimately—directly improving the general officers' ability to defeat the enemy.

Letterman's system was implemented gradually, from Second Manassas to Chancellorsville. He was pleased with the results:

> *It is well to remember that no system devised by man can be perfect, and that no such system, even if it existed,*

could be carried out perfectly by human agency. Calling to mind the fact that the ambulance system, imperfect as it may be found, could not be fully put into service—remembering the magnitude of the engagement, the length of time the battle lasted, and the obstinacy with which it was contested—it affords me much gratification to state that so few instances of apparently unnecessary suffering were found to exist after that action and that the wounded were removed from that sanguinary field in so careful and expeditious a manner.

Dr. Letterman had a right to be pleased. In July 1862, 37% of the Army of the Potomac was unable to report for duty due to sickness. A year later, the number had been reduced to 9%. The mortality rate of wounds dropped from 26% the first year to 15% and then 10% the next two years. Measured in human suffering, these results are nothing short of amazing.

Hospital flags made it easier for stretcher bearers and ambulance drivers to find field hospitals. They also served notice to enemy artillerists, who would typically avoid shelling a hospital as an act of mercy. (cm)

By the end of the war, every soldier could look forward to hearing, "It's okay. We've got you." A single credo always drove Letterman's thinking—the two things every soldier wants from the army are to be well fed and to know he will be taken care of if he falls wounded on the battlefield.

Dr. Jonathan Letterman, already known as "The Father of Battlefield Medicine," resigned his army commission in December 1864 due to illness and exhaustion. He relocated to San Francisco, California, where he practiced medicine and served as elected coroner from 1867 to 1872. In 1866, he published his Civil War memoirs, *Medical Recollections of the Army of the Potomac*. He died in March 1872, at the age of 48.

In 1911, the army hospital at San Francisco's Presidio was named in his honor. Letterman is buried next to his wife in Arlington National Cemetery. His headstone bears the following tribute: "Medical Director of the Army of the Potomac, June 23, 1862, to December 30, 1863, who brought order and efficiency into the Medical Service and who was the originator of modern methods of medical organization in armies."

At the National Museum of Civil War Medicine

The site most intimately related to Dr. Letterman's work is the National Museum of Civil War Medicine, in Frederick, Maryland—a three-site museum that also includes the Pry House Field Hospital in Antietam, Maryland (see Chapter Four), and the Clara Barton Missing Soldier Office in Washington, D. C. (more on her in Chapter Sixteen).

The Clara Barton Missing Soldier Office at 437 7th Street in Washington, D. C. (kd)

The Clara Barton Missing Soldier Office is the location where Clara Barton lived during the Civil War. Not only did she live in the rooms on 7th Street, she stored supplies necessary for her work on the battlefield there as well. After the war, she continued her residency, and her home became an office for correspondence concerning missing soldiers. More than 63,000 letters received her personal response. A tireless worker who left no lead unfollowed, she had identified the fate of over 22,000 men by 1867, including those who died at Georgia's Andersonville Prison.

The website containing information about this special piece of historic preservation is www.civilwarmed.org/clara-barton-museum/.

There are two short videos at the site. One is about Miss Barton herself and her efforts, and the founding of the Red Cross. The other is a tantalizing snippet concerning how the office itself was rediscovered during a scheduled demolition project to upgrade the Penn Quarter neighborhood. Both are well worth the less-than-ten minutes it takes to view them. Additionally, information concerning hours of operation may be found there as well.

The National Museum of Civil War Medicine is located at 48 E Patrick St in Frederick, Maryland. (cm)

The National Museum of Civil War Medicine ("Divided by Conflict, United by Compassion") offers much more, whether you are web browsing or planning a vacation. As stated, this museum is "the premier center for the preservation and research of the legacy of Civil War medical innovation and humanitarianism. As a living institution, we utilize artifacts. storytelling, and the historic lessons derived from that era to educate the public and define the impact on today's society."

They have, in the past, offered a History Lover's BBQ, featuring local wines, Civil War recipes, and a famous chef; a conference concerning Confederate hospitals featuring both prominent historians and medical professionals; and the Letterman Institute, which has dedicated itself to following in Dr. Letterman's footsteps and continuing to explore and demonstrate the relevance of applying historical perspective to modern challenges.

Every video clip available on this website is first rate in production values, information offered, and relevance. Especially moving is the discussion and demonstration concerning amputations. Civil War medicine is compared to modern medicine on the fields of Iraq and Afghanistan. The link to this part of the website is www.civilwarmed.org/letterman-institute/

NMCWM provides an on-line searchable database of artifacts from the Civil War era, which includes medical instruments and supplies, medical documents, personal correspondence, textbooks, and hospital items of the period. The site contains images of the majority of the NMCWM's collection. New acquisitions are regularly catalogued and added, and there is a link for the curator available for questions and the most current information. The link for this area of the site is www.civilwarmed.org/nmcwm-searchable-database-artifacts/.

If you're planning a trip to Frederick, Maryland, the NMCWM would be a wonderful addition to the agenda: www.civilwarmed.org/national-museum-of-civil-war-medicine/visit-us/

Unrelated to the NMCWM, but equally interesting, is the first medical museum in America: the Mütter Museum of Physicians in Philadelphia.

The Mütter, which celebrated its own sesquicentennial in 2013, displays its beautifully preserved collections of anatomical specimens, models, and medical instruments in a 19th century "cabinet museum" setting, allowing for a very unique museum experience for those who "dare" to enter its Victorian doors. The huge Mütter collection began as a donation from Dr. Thomas Dent Mütter, who was determined to improve and reform medical education. The goal of the Museum is to help the public understand the mysteries and beauty of the human body while appreciating the history of diagnosis and treatment of disease. Yes, it is sort of spooky.

The Mütter Museum of Physicians is located at 19 S. 22nd Street in Philadelphia, Pennsylvania. (mm)

The museum always houses interesting (and often interactive!) exhibits, and changes their topic on a regular basis. Be sure to check their website to see what is currently being featured: www.muttermuseum.org. Student-oriented lesson plans concerning Civil War medicine have been developed by the Museum. These can be accessed on the PA Commonwealth's Civil War website. Not only are there changing exhibits, there are permanent ones. Of particular interest to Civil War students is " 'This Dust Was Once a Man': The Final Days of Abraham Lincoln." This exhibit focuses on the injuries that Lincoln, Major Henry Rathbone, and John Wilkes Booth sustained during and after Lincoln's assassination. Some of Booth's thoracic tissue, personally delivered to the Pennsylvania College of Medicine after Booth's autopsy, is on display.

Well known in some circles, today the museum enjoys steadily rising international popularity, including a recent documentary on the Discovery Channel and two best-selling books.

Johnny Won't Be Marching Home

CHAPTER SEVEN

"The doctors were busy in probing for balls, binding up wounds, and in cutting off arms and legs, a pile of which lay under the table," wrote 18-year-old Alfred Bellard—and he should have known. Handsome young Alfred had heard the call of his president in 1861 and enlisted in the 5th New Jersey Volunteer Infantry. He proudly held the rank of "Private" at age 15. He accompanied the Army of the Potomac in many of its Virginia campaigns until the battle of Chancellorsville. Wounded in the leg, he endured the terrors of possible amputation as he lay in a field hospital near the battlefield.

When a drummer boy, brought from the camp, was operated on, Alfred witnessed the whole sad event. "I just picked up the gun to have a little fun," the drummer boy had reportedly said. "I held it in the fire, you see. . . ." All that was left of the drummer's hands after the gun exploded was a thumb on one hand and a finger and thumb on the other. Alfred wrote in his diary, "When the doctors had him on the table and under the influence of cloraform, they picked out the pieces of bone with their fingers."

Alfred described in his diary, published as *Gone For a Soldier*, the terrible scenes of severed arms and legs left under tables, in pits dug outside windows, and in traveling in lurching wheelbarrows. Amputation was one of the goriest medical byproducts of the Civil War. The aftermath of amputation had its own aftermath: the soldier had to try to recover from the surgery, and the body parts—they had to go somewhere, eventually.

Dr. Jonathan Letterman's makeshift Keedysville hospital, in Maryland, was typical of how a Civil War era hospital operating theater was organized. When the wounded arrived from the Antietam battlefield in September 1862, the worst cases were taken to a brick church near the northern end of town. Letterman's

Poet Walt Whitman wrote one of the war's most famous scenes about amputation when he visited the field hospital at Chatham Manor following the battle of Fredericksburg. "Outdoors, at the foot of a tree, within ten yards of the front of the house, I noticed a heap of amputated feet, legs, arms, hands, etc.—about a load for a one-horse cart." The tree still stands. (cm)

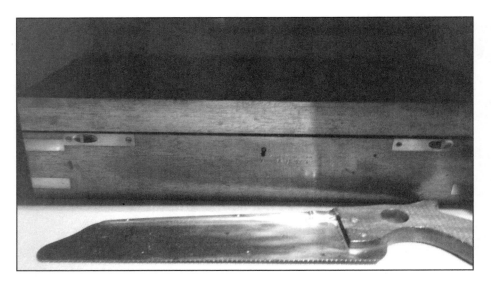

This bone saw, on display at the Fredericksburg Battlefield Visitor Center, is typical of the type used by surgeons for amputations. Such saws were standard equipment in a doctor's field kit. (CM)

memoirs describe how boards were laid across the backs of the pews to create elevated platforms. These were then covered with straw and blankets. "Comrades with wounds of all conceivable shapes were brought in and placed side by side as thick as they could lay, and the bloody work of amputation commenced." A pit was dug under the window at the back of the church and, "as soon as a limb was amputated, [an orderly] would take it to the window and drop it outside into the pit."

"Doc! Doc! Ya gotta help me here!" remembered hospital orderly George Allen of the 76th New York Infantry. The man whose voice commanded Letterman's attention was a soldier who had just endured the loss of his hand to the bone saw. Nevertheless, the patient complained to the doctor that the phantom hand was "all cramped up and hurting mighty bad." Letterman motioned to orderly Allen, who walked outside and around to the back of the church. He "fished out the hand" for its former owner, and brought it back to Letterman. With care, Allen straightened out the hand and then offered it to the soldier. As soon as the patient saw it, "he complained no more of the pain in the stump."

Tiny, dark-haired Miss Jane Moore, a volunteer nurse who worked at Gettysburg with the XII Corps primarily, wrote her own version of amputation horrors. "Shrieks, cries, and groans resounded on all sides, not only from those in the tents but on the amputating tables, which were almost constantly occupied," she wrote; "and who could pass them without a dreadful shudder at those ghastly bleeding limbs heaped without, which the eye, however cautious, could not always avoid."

Even the average soldier got used to seeing things

formerly unimaginable. An unknown soldier from the battle of Fredericksburg wrote in a letter home after seeing bushel baskets of amputated limbs being removed from the field hospital, "one gets used to such seens quicker than you would think it possible."

On the Bentonville battlefield in North Carolina, Surgeon Waldo Daniels used the Harper House as his field hospital. (dd)

Often the practice of post-battle amputations was criticized. It left men disfigured, and minus a limb that might be necessary to employment after the war. Some characterized it as butchery by poorly trained surgeons, but Letterman did not agree. "It is not to be supposed that there were no incompetent surgeons in the army," he defended. "These sweeping denunciations against a class of men who will favorably compare with the military surgeons of any country . . . are wrong."

The damage done by canister and shot from artillery, and from a minié ball shot from a rifled weapon, may be compared to the damage done today by exploding bullets and roadside explosives. Amputation gave a severely wounded patient his best chance at survival.

Not all survived, though. Surgeon Franklin Hough wrote to his family of the "house of death" a hospital becomes at night. "On the litter lies a man whose leg has been nearly torn from his body by a shell; he looks up into your face . . . and mildly asks, 'Will it kill me?' If you must answer that the wound is fatal, he closes his eyes; you see his lips moving in prayer . . . hear him feebly imploring protection and care for his poor wife and children, 'Tell them I have done my duty faithfully as a good soldier and my last wish was for their welfare.'"

The vast majority of the amputated limbs were simply burned and the ashes dug into the ground. This was the same procedure used for dead animals, and it was the

Piles of amputated limbs, gruesome as they were, were a common sight at field hospitals in the wake of major battles. (mg)

quickest and most sanitary way to dispose of the hundreds of pounds of remains that had nowhere else to go.

There were a couple of interesting exceptions, though: Dan Sickles's leg and Stonewall Jackson's arm. Both have interesting stories of their own to tell.

*   *   *

Another particularly compelling use of dead bodies began in earnest on April 28, 1862. This was the date when big, bright, annoying Dr. William A. Hammond was officially appointed surgeon general of the U.S. Army. On May 21 of the same year, Circular No. 2 was issued, and changed American medicine forever. Circular No. 2 directed all army medical officers to "diligently collect and forward to the office of the Surgeon General all specimens of morbid anatomy . . . which may be regarded as valuable; together with projectiles and foreign bodies removed . . ." Never before had a country had access to the remains of so many dead men, and never before had science advanced to the point where so much could be learned from the remains. American medicine veered quickly to the left, and began to create a new structure for medical advancement.

Hammond graduated from medical school at 20 years old. From 1849 to 1860, he was an assistant surgeon in the Federal army. He served in the western posting of New Mexico, removing an occasional arrowhead and attending to the soldiers' chronic dehydration and heatstroke. In 1860, when he was offered a job at the University of Maryland as chair of their Anatomy and Physiology Department, Hammond moved his growing family to Baltimore. All went well until war was declared and a unit of Federal soldiers was physically attacked as they moved through Baltimore on their way to Washington. Hammond treated the soldiers in the Baltimore Infirmary, and within six weeks he was back in the army.

An ambitious, smart, and fearless man like William Hammond caused more trouble than then-Surgeon General Clement Finley thought he was worth, so Hammond was transferred to the Army of the Cumberland, under Maj. Gen. William Rosecrans. It was there that Hammond met Letterman. They immediately formed a friendship and began working on putting some finishing touches on Letterman's new designs for Union ambulances. Surgeon General Finley argued with Secretary of War William Stanton and lost his job. Against all precedence, President Abraham Lincoln appointed the politically connected Hammond in his place, granting him the rank of brigadier general.

Hammond's record of reforms is filled with things taken for granted today, but were very innovative for their time, including hiring and promotion based on talent and worth as opposed to seniority within the army's Medical Department. Most important to the subject of the disposal of human military remains is that Hammond founded the Army Medical Museum, now called the National Museum of Health and Medicine. Circular No. 2 demanded that to this museum should be sent the hundreds of thousands of legs, arms, knees, ankles, hands, shoulders, and complete corpses—packed in ice or in barrels of whiskey or alcohol.

Each specimen that arrived was immediately tagged and catalogued. Whenever possible, slides were made with the help of a relatively new instrument in the medical arsenal—the microscope. Additionally, autopsies began to be done regularly on those who died in hospitals. Finally, the war doctors of the Union Army were at the forefront of this type of collective investigation.

The results were almost immediate. It was soon clear that the overall health of the Union Army was poor, contributing as much as anything to the large numbers of casualties who eventually died. Much more accurate information about blood vessels and arties increased the chances for a successful resection of almost any body part. Bits of bone were pieced back together to create better, more informed decisions about the efficacy of amputation.

Dr. C. Wagner, a physician serving in one of the military hospitals surrounding Washington, included a brief note with one group of specimens to arrive at the museum. He not only described what he had sent in the current barrel, but asked the museum to anticipate "one very pretty specimen, a portion of the cranium from a case of resection of the cranium."

Case after case arrived at the museum, and American doctors were quick to see its advantages in furthering the standards of care for wartime patients, and for extending this knowledge beyond the war. Letterman wrote to Hammond in support of the entire enterprise: "It always affords me pleasure to cooperate with you in any way possible to advance the interests of the museum. . . . I shall be glad to cooperate with you in any way in my power to amass something out of the dying in this war."

In antebellum America, states had laws (anatomy acts) in place to cover the disposal of human remains. Much effort was expended to return a body to its family, if possible. By the time the war became a sad reality, many of these laws had been repealed. This opened up to doctors and scientists a freer atmosphere for dissection and exploratory autopsy. There was an important and unprecedented dimension to the wartime treatment of bodies: by expanding medical knowledge through dissection, those still living and fighting had a greater chance of being saved, a final sacrifice to the cause of Union.

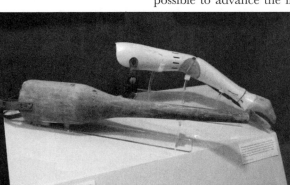

The development of prosthetic limbs became much more sophisticated in the wake of the Civil War because demand was so high. (nmcwm)

Dr. John H. Brinton, the first curator of the Army Medical Museum, was asked to give a speech to the graduating class of the Army Medical School in 1896. He told his story, remembering the decisions of a group of young soldiers concerning the disposition of the remains of a good friend. The soldier had sustained a terrible leg wound, which was immediately pronounced "rare" and was carefully studied by the army surgeons. Unfortunately, the man died and was buried by his friends in "soldier fashion." Not willing to let anything be left to chance, the friends sat up with their buried companion until the "nefarious collector" arrived. "Boys," the collector began:

> It is so nice to see such a dedicated group of friends. I am willing to bet that this soldier was dedicated to all of you, as well as to his country. This is a terrible war, and it takes too many too soon. But there is still one more sacrifice your pard can still give—that leg of his. It may seem like just another leg wound to you, but to a trained eye, maybe someone else could see more. Maybe even could see how to keep such a wound from being fatal, as it was to our late companion now lying in his grave. Patriotic bones rest better in a medical case than in a trench in Virginia.

So great was the earnestness, the sympathy, and the

eloquence of the doctor who had come to retrieve the leg that the hearts of the soldiers softened. They stood by while the corpse was exhumed and the leg removed. One of the friends of the deceased soldier remarked that, "after all, John would rather be of some use to the very end."

So what happened to all the body parts remaining in the aftermath of battle? Most were simply burned and then interred as ash and bits of bone. But many found their way to the doctors of the Army Medical Museum, becoming part of the vast storehouse of knowledge compiled with the one aim of saving soldier lives. Was it successful? In the European-based Franco-Prussian War, begun in 1870, the mortality rate for amputations was a staggering 76 percent. In contrast, for almost 30,000 amputations recorded in the Union army, the mortality rate was 26.3 percent. These amazing results can be placed directly on the marble stairs of the Army Medical Museum, its doctors, and the soldiers who gave beyond their "last, full measure."

At the National Museum of Health and Medicine

One of the most famous curiosities of the Civil War—the amputated leg of Daniel Sickles, lost at the battle of Gettysburg—is one of the many fascinating exhibits at the National Museum of Health and Medicine. Established during the Civil War as the Army Medical Museum, it was the repository for specimens collected from many Civil War battlegrounds. Surgeons and medical officers were ordered by Surgeon General William Hammond to collect these "specimens of morbid anatomy together with projectiles and foreign bodies" carefully from the field and operating tent. They were then sent to the museum, in hopes that studying them might improve medical care for wounded soldiers.

The National Museum of Health and Medicine is located at 2500 Linden Lane, Silver Spring, Maryland. (oha)

John Brinton was actively sending specimens back to Washington from the battlefields. He received help from many other army doctors. In addition to collecting bones, the Museum staff photographed many wounded soldiers, graphically recording the effects of battlefield wounds, amputations, and other surgical procedures. This information was compiled into a six-volume set entitled The Medical and Surgical History of the War of the Rebellion, published between 1870 and 1883.

Information online may be found at www.wmata.com.

From the Battlefield to Home

CHAPTER EIGHT

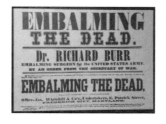

There was no piped-in music on May 25, 1861. The dry murmur of silk and the creak and shuffle of shoe leather, combined with the low voices, created a sound as familiar at a funeral as the scent of lilies, garden roses, and white trillium. Hundreds of people walked past the rosewood casket with the oval viewing window to look upon the face of young Col. Elmer Ellsworth. Mary Lincoln, the wife of President Abraham Lincoln, had planned the event. Dr. Thomas Holmes, a medical doctor who worked in Washington City, offered his services as an embalmer. He was one of the few practitioners who did arsenic embalming. Mary Lincoln took him up on his offer.

The Lincolns looked down into the pale face of their friend. "He looks as natural as though he were sleeping a brief and pleasant sleep," Mary commented sadly. The embalmer had done an excellent job. President Lincoln was impressed as well: later, he requested Holmes's services for their 11-year old son, Willie Lincoln, when the boy died on February 20, 1862, of typhoid fever. In 1865, Mrs. Lincoln once again asked for Dr. Holmes when the President himself was assassinated.

Before the Civil War, bodies had rarely been embalmed. Death occurred at home, or at sea, or no one cared. Graves were dug and remains were buried in wooden coffins, letting Nature take her course. In case a large number of deaths occurred in a similar geographic area, mass graves were dug and bodies dumped in without a great deal of ceremony. After the catastrophe—illness or weather-related, usually—things could be sorted out.

By the middle of the nineteenth century, the search

"Furniture and undertaking" seem like an odd business combination, but carpentry was an essential skill for coffin making. (nmcwm)

for a safe but antiseptic embalming solution had become an item of health concern, and the coming of the Civil War made an effective embalming method a priority.

The science of embalming has been around since the Egyptians. Essentially, it involves the removal and replacement of blood with some sort of liquid preservative. Many different chemical combinations were tried, including vinegar and grain alcohol, but early attempts had mixed results. Bodies often began to decompose before burial, especially if they had to be sent any distance.

Of course, many soldiers died far from their homes. Their frantic families pressed for a way to preserve the remains—if there were any—for the journey from the hospital or battlefield to wherever *home* was. It did not seem right for a young man to simply disappear, but a large number of them did just that.

Dr. Thomas Holmes, a well-respected graduate of Columbia University's Medical School, developed a method of preserving bodies that included the intra-arterial injection of an arsenic-based embalming fluid. As America moved steadily toward war, Holmes quickly realized the commercial potential of embalming and moved his successful practice to Washington. He handed out thousands of fliers to soldiers who had joined the war effort, offering to preserve their bodies in case of death. In 1861, when Virginia ratified its letters of secession, Holmes approached the U.S. government to obtain exclusive rights to embalm Union soldiers so they could be shipped home for burial. His efforts at self-promotion paid off, and started the course of events that made the attempted preservation of remains a common practice.

By the time the war had started in earnest, the

embalming tent was a battlefield staple. Not all dead soldiers were embalmed. Statistically only about six percent of them were. Embalming surgeons traveled from site to site looking for the dead and pumping a mixture of arsenic and other chemicals into their veins, which delayed the decaying process. Most charged around $7 for enlisted men and $13 for officers.

These embalmers were often accused of extortion and dubious practices. Not only did they hover around the departed like vultures, they often unfairly charged for their services. A Yankee news reporter related one conversation with a particularly enterprising embalmer. "I would be glad to prepare private soldiers. They were worth a five dollar bill apiece," the embalmer said:

> But, Lord bless you, a colonel pays a hundred, and a brigadier-general two hundred. There's lots of them now, and I have cut the acquaintance of everything below a major. I might, as a great favor, do a captain, but he must pay a major's price. I insist upon that! Such windfalls don't come every day. There won't be another such killing for a century.

Embalming was a much rarer occurrence in the Confederacy than in the North, but Northern embalmers advertised in Southern newspapers, pointing out the convenience of their newly opened "field offices" on the site of recent battles. Embalmer and medical doctor William Maclure promised "persons at a distance" that "BODIES OF THE DEAD" would be "Disinterred, Disinfected, and SENT HOME" from any place within the Confederacy.

There were other well-known embalmers besides Dr. Holmes. Dr. F. A. Hutton advertised that "Bodies embalmed by us NEVER TURN BLACK!" Dr. William J. Bunnell's embalming tent did a grand business after the battle of Fredericksburg, embalming as many as 100 men a day. Dr. Richard Burr was a battlefield embalmer, as were doctors C. B. Chamberlain and Benjamin F. Lyford. Burr, from Philadelphia, was a good example of a bad embalmer. He was well known for his price gouging and for selling and reselling the same grave marker for locally buried soldiers. His method of arterial embalming used an artery in the armpit rather than the carotid artery. This method was faster, easier, and left almost no marks on the body. It bypassed the filling of the abdominal cavity altogether. After all, with corpses piled up at the door, speed was of the essence.

In the South, doctors Sampson and George Diuguid, of Lynchburg, Virginia, ran the oldest mortuary in the Confederacy. Founded in 1817 by the Diuguid family, it was responsible for the burials and embalming of over 3,000 soldiers, both Union and Confederate. Their business had begun long before the war, and the record-keeping processes concerning each body were already firmly established. Accurate records were kept for every burial or removal during the war. Each body was documented, listing name, place of death, date of burial, military unit, and place of burial, along with coffin and body measurements. These records proved invaluable when, after the war, the Federal government wished to remove the remains of more than 200 soldiers for reburial in the National Cemetery near Petersburg.

One particularly interesting embalmer was Prince Greer, America's first African American embalmer. He was the personal slave of a Confederate cavalry officer who was killed in Tennessee. Greer took it upon himself to return the body of his former master to his estate and contacted a Nashville undertaker, Dr. W. P. Cornelius, for help in this endeavor. Cornelius embalmed the officer, and his body was shipped back to Texas, but during this time Cornelius's assistant decided that embalming was not quite the job he wanted. Upon the departure of the assistant, Prince Greer stepped forward. He offered to learn the embalming trade in exchange for room and board, and Cornelius was glad to have him:

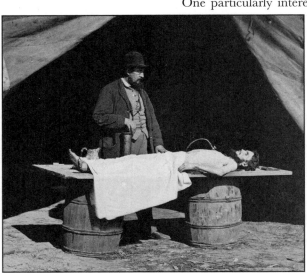

In a scene that might have come out of *Frankenstein*, an embalmer works to preserve a corpse by feeding chemicals into the body. (loc)

> *Prince Greer appeared to enjoy embalming so much that he himself became an expert, kept on at work embalming during the balance of the war and was very successful at it. It was but a short time before he could raise an artery as quickly as anyone. He was always careful, always . . . coming to me in a difficult case. He remained with me until I quit the business in 1871.*

So many complaints regarding the embalmers who followed the Union army were made that, on January 9, 1865, Gen. Ulysses S. Grant finally issued General Order No. 7, from City Point, Virginia:

> *All embalming surgeons having been excluded from the lines of the armies operating against Richmond, the*

Dr. William J. Bunnell made a show of his work in order to take advantage of people's morbid curiosity. (loc)

friends and relatives of the officers and soldiers are hereby notified that hereafter the bodies of officers and soldiers who die in general or base hospitals can be embalmed without charge upon making personal application to the chief medical officer of the hospitals. Applications for the embalming of officers and soldiers who die at division hospitals at the front or on the field of battle must be made to the medical director of the corps to which such officers or soldiers belonged. By command of Lieutenant-General Grant: T. S. Bowers, Assistant Adjutant-General.

Federal War Department General Order No. 39, issued March 15, 1865, followed Grant's admonition. It insisted that all embalmers be licensed by the local military Provost Marshal, demanded that disinterment be restricted to appropriate seasons, and fixed prices for services.

*   *   *

In contrast to the lack of ceremony surrounding the disposition of the dead on or near fields of battle, conditions in Union camps and hospitals allowed for more conventional burial practices that maintained earlier traditions. Reasons for this difference had nothing to do with the smaller numbers of dying soldiers in these settings. More men died from disease than wounds inflicted in battle, so there were ample numbers of corpses to be buried. Camps and hospitals simply had more resources, personnel, and time to take care of these matters. Many also had space singled out for use as cemeteries, which provided a readily available and organized location for disposal.

Miss Louisa May Alcott was a nurse in Washington. "I . . . hurried back to him," she wrote of one of her patients. "He seemed asleep; but something in the tired white face caused me to listen at his lips for a breath. None

This ice coffin, on display at the National Civil War Chaplains Museum in Lynchburg, Virginia, shows the horse-hair insulation that helped keep a body cold during transport. (cm)

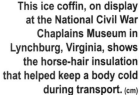

came. . . . I knew that . . . a better nurse than I had given him a cooler draught, and healed him with a touch." Of another, she remembered, "I had cut some brown locks of hair for his mother, and taken off the ring to send her . . . laid the letter in his hand, feeling that its place was there, and making myself happy with the thought that, even in his solitary grave in the 'Government Lot,' he would not be without some token of love. . . ."

Regimental hospitals much closer to battlefields could not offer the kind of attention that larger hospitals provided the dead. Descriptions of death and dying in these locations can be found in a number of soldiers' letters and diaries, anticipating the shifting scenery of expiration from home to hospital. The presence of corpses, as well as other reminders of human mortality like piles of amputated limbs, did not evoke images of order and solemnity. Instead, death and burial had many of the same characteristics found on fields of battle, though a rudimentary graveyard next to these hospitals allowed for a slightly more organized space for disposing of remains.

For family members and friends in the North, the prospect of loved ones dying far away from home and being interred in what most considered to be profane Southern soil led to a great deal of anguish and outrage. Many Northerners were deeply disturbed by this prospect because it upset the social script ingrained in American culture when a family experienced a death. Some families, particularly the more affluent families in the North, would do whatever they could to bring the body of a loved family member's home, either by making the trip south on their own, or paying someone to locate, retrieve, and ship the body north.

As a result of these desires—to maintain familial control over the final resting place and, if possible, to have one last look at their loved one—a new form of

According to the National Museum of Civil War Medicine, "Holding coffins contained metal trays above and below the body, which when filled with ice, preserved the body until embalming or burial. The grillwork upon which the body would rest has a wooden support on which the head of the deceased would rest. Viewing took place through a hatch above the face. These coffins were usually only available for rent in larger cities, not rural areas. Upon burial the body was placed in a permanent coffin." (nmcwm)

treating the dead appeared, and paved the way for the birth of an entirely modern funeral industry.

Undertakers who contracted with Northern families began to experiment with innovative means to preserve bodies that had to be shipped long distances on train cars, often during the hot summer months. The revolutionary practice that emerged in this context, embalming, provided both the military and Northern communities with a scientific, sanitary, and sensible way to move bodies across the land.

For most, however, this was not possible. Much as families wished to offer their loved ones a funeral like Elmer Ellsworth's, there were now far too many dead for that to be realistic. Poet Walt Whitman described the most common way in which many soldiers were buried:

> *The graves with slight boards, rudely inscribed with*
> *   the names,*
> *The front of the hospital, the dead brought out,*
> *   lying there so still,*
> *The piece of board, hastily inscribed with the name,*
> *   placed on the breast to be ready,*
> *The squad at the burial, firing a volley over the grave.*

Unless, of course, an individual soldier's final resting place was unknown . . . as so many were.

All Was Confusion

CHAPTER NINE

JULY 5, 1863

The night of July 3 was one long, terrible nightmare for those in the Union field hospital behind Cemetery Ridge. Fighting earlier in the day seemed to be the worst ever, and now, the line for the chief surgeon's amputating table appeared endless, packed with almost as many men in gray as in blue. The grinding of the bone saw dulled the hearing of those in close proximity to the moans and repeated cries of injured soldiers.

Then, slowly, one voice rose above the hellish din. It was a female voice, a sweet soprano with some degree of training. Standing on a bloody wooden table was a short, slightly dumpy woman of twenty-seven years: Miss Helen Gilson, one of the nurses and the only woman in the hospital.

Blood smeared her apron. Her hands were wiped only a bit cleaner, but she held them steady. Gently she urged the men to join her as she sang: hymns almost every man in America had learned in childhood. The well-known tunes spoke of home and loved ones.

Slowly the voices gathered strength. Wounded men scratched and whispered out the words, while the surgeons muttered them under their breath—truly a chorus of the macabre. By the time Gilson began to sing "Battle Hymn of the Republic," the strange choir she led followed her note for note.

Helen Gilson was not the only woman on the battlefield in those days after the battle of Gettysburg. Father Francis Burlando came with fourteen Sisters of Charity from the

The bas-relief plaque on the front of St. Xavier's Church strikes a note of reconciliation: "During the battle of Gettysburg, this House of God became a hospital for wounded soldiers. Within its hallowed walls brave men of North and South, foes on the field of battle, through weeks of pain were nursed with tender and equal care by the Sisters of Charity of Emmitsburg." (cm)

"The roar of these agents of death and destruction was fearful in the extreme," wrote Father Francis Burlando, describing the battle of Gettysburg, "and their smoke rising to heaven formed dense clouds as during a frightful tempest. The Army of the South was defeated and in their retreat left their dead and wounded on the battlefield." (cwt)

convent in nearby Emmitsburg. These nursing sisters were veterans of Antietam, but even that did not prepare them for the shock of so much carnage, nor for the eerie quiet of the morning of July 5. Sister Marie Louise Caufield remarked later that it seemed, "as silent almost as the dead that lay by the hundreds on the ground."

Gettysburg resident Fannie J. Beuhler wrote that she could see from her house on Baltimore Street, dead soldiers "all lying in the streets, so far as we could see, either up or down."

Many who experienced the battle, either as participants or onlookers, took pains to mention that the entire part of the population that was ambulatory wandered aimlessly, dazed and incredulous at the carnage, not knowing what to do or where to go.

"Tension was everywhere, all was confusion," said Mother Superior Ann Simpson Norris, who added that the residents appeared as "frightened ghosts, so terrified had they been during the battle."

It was the scope of the destruction that left so many so appalled. In town, every church pew, every bed, every barn, every alley and street held a full share of wounded men, many of whom were mortally hurt. Out at the battlefield—all 25 square miles of it—the dead outnumbered the living, and were found in every nook and cranny imaginable. Some were up trees, some were wedged among rocks, some lay where they had fallen, in front of the Round Tops, along the rows of the Peach Orchard, stacked at the Angle like more fencing. It appeared as if the rain of July 4 had been a downpour of dead soldiers instead of water.

The battle of Gettysburg was fought on July 1-3, 1863, in and around the small college town in Adams County, Pennsylvania. Union Maj. Gen. George Gordon Meade's Army of the Potomac defeated Lee's Army of Northern Virginia in a battle that involved the largest number of casualties of the entire war.

Before the battle began on July 1, Meade's army was well supplied with doctors, assistants, medical supplies, and tents to assist the wounded. The ambulance corps travelled with the army at all times. Meade's medical director, Dr. Jonathan Letterman, was up-to-date on all the newest ways to save lives and prevent suffering that were available mid-century. He had put measures in place for collecting the wounded and bringing them in for care. His methods had worked well at Chancellorsville earlier in the year, and he was quietly confident in their success now—except for one small matter.

On June 19, then-commander of the Army of the Potomac Maj. Gen. Joseph Hooker had ordered a reduction in the number of medical supply wagons in order to move the army faster in its effort to pursue the invading Confederates through Virginia. The number had gone from six wagons per division to two.

Letterman did what he could to salvage the situation by creating a reserve supply train in Washington. When he realized that battle was imminent, Letterman telegraphed to have the wagons brought up to Westminster, about 20 miles from Gettysburg. They arrived on the eve of battle, but an already-bad situation was made worse when Meade ordered his corps commanders to send all wagons except ammunition and ambulances to the rear. This meant that there were very few medical supplies within 20 miles of where they were going to be desperately needed. "Without proper means, the Medical Department can no more take care of the wounded than the army can fight a battle without ammunition," complained Dr. Letterman, to no avail. "Lost supplies can be replenished, but lives lost are gone forever."

In particular, there were no large canvas tents available to shelter wounded men from the elements. Most of the casualties lay in the wet, muddy ground with no cover save what could be improvised from branches and clothing. They were not concealed from either the battle or the scenes of horror unfolding around them. Surgeons had to work in the open air, with no protection from sun or rain for anyone.

After the battle but before the Army of the Potomac pulled out to follow the Army of Northern Virginia, Meade contracted with local residents to organize groups of able-bodies citizens, mostly African-American, to bury the dead. Coffins were made quickly out of anything that came to hand, including doors and furniture, but there were nowhere near enough.

Pennsylvania militia members were pressed into

Inside St. Xavier's Church, a stained glass window commemorates the post-battle acts of mercy performed by the Sisters of Charity. (dw)

service as burial details. Many of the bodies had been left to decompose for several days and needed careful handling in order to remain intact. Often they were shoveled onto boards, and then dumped into shallow graves, one after the other. Some were dragged by their belts, or moved with bayonets, rakes, or pitchforks. In addition to the more than 7,000 dead, there were more than 33,000 wounded in the battle—more than 14,500 Northerners and 19,000 Southerners. Meade had left only 106 medical officers behind to care for these men.

Battlefield photography brought the war to northern doorsteps in graphic ways; the battle of Gettysburg brought the war to northern doorsteps in a whole new way entirely. (loc)

One part of the battlefield was worse than the next, both during and after the battle. The rear of Cemetery Ridge, where the Union Second Corps was established, not only had to deal with its own casualties, but also with those of the Confederate forces that attacked the Union center on July 3. Twenty-three-year-old Cornelia Hancock, a patriotic, gently-reared Quaker, had come from New Jersey to help in any way she could. She wrote that she saw, "a collection of semi-conscious but still living human forms, all of whom had been shot through the head, and were considered hopeless. They were laid there to die and I hoped that they were indeed too near death to have consciousness."

Burial of the dead took weeks. (loc)

Gettysburg was a Union victory, so Northern soldiers received care first. Southern soldiers were not purposefully treated callously—hundreds were moved to higher ground when in danger of drowning in the torrential rains of July 4, and several southern women came northward to tend the wounded, although it took them a few days to arrive. Lee left his wounded to be tended by 10 surgeons and more than 150 nurses, attendants, and cooks. He had taken as many as 8,000 wounded with him. Not only were the Confederates short of personnel, they had practically no medical supplies. Hopeful that the Union could make up this deficit, the Southern surgeons were disappointed. There was little that could be done to relieve the misery of the Union soldiers until more help and supplies arrived, and at first it was a toss-up as to which side got better or faster treatment.

Confederate Lt. John Dooley sustained two serious leg wounds. He was treated at the Union Corps Second Hospital behind Cemetery Ridge, and wrote:

> *The whole ground for miles around is covered with the wounded, the dying, and the dead. Confederate and Yankee are often . . . thrown together, although the officials often separate us generally as much as is convenient. The Yankees are nearly all comfortably quartered, having tents and blankets and many little comforts which they have . . . received from their comrades. This is only natural and none of our boys expect to receive attentions in preference to the enemy's wounded.*

One reason for the discrepancy in comforts was simply that the Union army provided shelter halves to their soldiers as a matter of course, while Confederate soldiers usually carried a bedroll and slept on the ground.

Even more pressing than the need for medical supplies and shelter was the need for food. On July 4, 30,000 rations had been issued, but thousands never saw food or water of any type for several days after the battle.

Although the number of deaths at Gettysburg is high (more than 51,000), it would have been much higher had not both the U.S. Sanitary Commission and the U.S. Christian Commission arrived when they did. The Sanitary Commission was a group of volunteers who helped organize the entire North into various soldier aid societies. Both groups created an effective conduit for civilian donations of goods and money to flow almost immediately to the men in the field.

To help those soldiers who could be evacuated, a Relief Lodge was established on July 7 where the railroad bridge over Rock Creek was down. The bridge was rebuilt and service was restored on July 10, and during those days, good beef soup, coffee, and fresh bread was provided for

The Fahnestock brothers' dry goods store (above) in downtown Gettysburg was used by the United States Sanitary Commission as a storehouse for the vast amount of materials necessary to tend to the large number of wounded who remained in town after both armies moved out. The building, located at the corner of Middle and Baltimore streets, still stands (top). (loc)(cm)

All of Gettysburg's churches, like Christ Lutheran on West High Street, were used as hospitals in the aftermath of battle. (cm)

more than 3,000 slightly wounded soldiers whose injuries did not prevent them from walking the trains. They came limping, dragging themselves along, silent, weary, and worn. Two large tents, capable of sheltering 75 men, were pitched, stoves erected and the lodge established. Once the rail line was restored to the depot in town, a larger Relief Lodge was established adjacent to it.

Thousands of bodies lay, blackened, festering, and bloating in the sun and rain. Both Commissions quickly set up their own establishments at large stores owned by local Gettysburg families. They worked tirelessly, unceasingly, to give aid and succor to the wounded. Supplies began to be more plentiful, but the shortage of food continued. One of the most popular innovations of the Christian Commission was their Coffee Wagon, which could brew 108 gallons of coffee an hour—welcome brew to so many. They provided the extra aid necessary to help the overworked nurses and surgeons to provide care for more than 21,000 seriously wounded men. Many of these men would have died without this added assistance. Neither Union nor Confederate government was able to administer this situation successfully. An editorial in the Adams *Sentinel* eloquently said that both agencies "have been doing noble work here. The thousands of wounded men . . . will ever bear in kind remembrance the untiring efforts of the Commissions."

*   *   *

As soon as the trains could reach Gettysburg, the town experienced another invasion. This one was mainly made up of five types of people: those who came to help, those who came to search for loved ones, those who came to profit (morticians, embalmers, coffin-makers, etc.), relic hunters, and finally those who simply came to satisfy their curiosity, however morbid it might be. These last arrived, dressed in their nicest clothes, ready to stare, gawk, gasp, and exclaim over the morbid, ghastly sights—and then go back home. These visitors put an even greater strain on the little burg. There was no place to put anyone, and many simply wandered the streets all night. What little food there was had been reserved for the soldiers.

Sightseers were not the only battlefield ghouls. A *New York Herald* writer saw "a country man engaged in cutting the harness from one of the dead battery horses, and preparing to carry it away from the field. Another has collected a dozen blankets, dropped by soldiers in the heat of the engagement. Another walks past me with three of the best muskets he can find. . . ."

With its neat rows of tents and clear protocols, Camp Letterman brought a sense of order to the post-battle chaos. (loc)

In fact, battlefield detritus seemed to litter the entire landscape. Another journalist, this one from the rival *New York Times*, described the area as being "covered with rifles, bayonets, blankets, cartridge-boxes, clothing, etc. and thousands of dollars worth of it are being carried off daily by those visiting the scene of the conflict."

The report of Provost Marshal Marsena Patrick noted angrily that one organized effort at stealing involved "a number of nondescript scavengers" who made money by selling rags to a paper mill. They came in teams, day and night, to loot dead soldiers. "They even resurrected corpses from their shallow entombment in the hope that some valuable might be found on the festering body."

"A sickening, overpowering, awful stench announced the presence of the unburied dead, on which the July sun was mercilessly shining . . ." wrote Cornelia Hancock, "and at every step the air grew heavier and fouler, until it seemed to possess a palpable horrible density that could be seen and felt and cut with a knife. The deadly, nauseating atmosphere robbed the battlefield of its glory, the survivors of its victory." And for some reason—

volunteer, sightseer, or battlefield scavenger—they all came in spite of the smell.

* * *

Patients at Camp Letterman assembled for a photo prior to the camp's closure. (loc)

By fall, stock could be taken with much more satisfactory results. Camp Letterman, the final field hospital at Gettysburg, closed on November 20, 1863. The battlefield had been mostly cleared, and the less-severely wounded had been sent to hospitals like Philadelphia's Satterlee General Hospital or Mower General Hospital. The Daughters of Charity handed their charges off to the Sisters of Mercy in Pittsburgh. Thousands of men had been saved, nursed, or buried. Who could say what had made the difference? Was it the food sent to the hospitals or the hands that served it? Was it the saw of a surgeon or the cheer and support of comrades? Perhaps it was the sum of all the massive, superhuman efforts made by so many that brought the living up toward the day and gently covered the dead with eternal night. But then, no one ever knows who pulls off a miracle.

Sister Marie Louise Caufield, one of the Catholic sisters who arrived with Father Burlando, wrote eloquently about the scenes that had greeted her as she and her sisters first arrived at the battlefield. "The rain had filled the roads with water, and here it was red with blood," she wrote. "Our horses could hardly be made to proceed on account of the horrid objects lying about them."

The aftermath of a terrible three-day battle—the bodies, the detritus, the lonely hopelessness and pain—all had been bound up as well as possible by hands both trained and untrained. Gettysburg had affected the entire nation, North and South.

At Gettysburg

There are many books and pamphlets written to help a visitor unravel the monuments and statues that now make up the Gettysburg battlefield. Purchasing one or two of these is a good investment, as is joining in on a program offered by National Park Service historians or a battlefield tour offered by the Association of Licensed Battlefield Guides.

Everything necessary to know in order to plan a trip to Gettysburg, Pennsylvania, can be found on the Gettysburg National Park website, at: www.nps.gov/gett/index.htm. Evergreen Cemetery is still an active cemetery and crematorium. Information concerning this location may be found at www.evergreencemetery.org.

Something a bit more off the beaten path might include:

St. Francis Xavier Church:

This church became a battlefield hospital after the battle of Gettysburg and was staffed by Roman Catholic nuns. Soldiers of both the Union and the Confederacy were equally attended to with spiritual and medical care. The lovely stained glass windows in the church show scenes of the wounded soldiers under the care of their sister-nurses. St. Francis Church traditionally holds an outdoor field Mass commemorating the dead and wounded.

The historic church's address is 25 West High Street, and the St. Pope John Paul II Chapel is at 455 Table Rock Road. Please check the parish website for information concerning access to the church and Mass schedules: www.www.stfxcc.org.

St. Xavier's Church (cm)

Camp Letterman Marker:

In a particularly startling instance of "lack of historical respect," the marker for Camp Letterman is across the street from the McDonald's on Route 30 East. This is all that remains of the largest, most effective field hospital ever built: Camp Letterman. The hospital was set up by order of Dr. Jonathan Letterman on July 5, 1863. It was located on the farm of George Wolfe, located on the York Pike.

Hundreds of tents were at the site for the wounded, supplies, and surgery. A morgue and cemetery were also put in place. There were more than 1,200 burials at the camp. The Union dead were removed in 1864 and re-buried in the new national cemetery while the Confederate dead were relocated over the years to cemeteries in the South. By November 1863 only a few patients remained at the camp. The camp was closed shortly thereafter.

Camp Letterman marker (cm)

The site of Camp Letterman has long since been paved and converted into a shopping center. (dd)

The Last Full Measure

CHAPTER TEN

NOVEMBER 19, 1863

President Lincoln was coming to Gettysburg. A National Soldiers' Cemetery had been proposed, accepted, and was now going to be dedicated. Initially the ceremony was to be on October 23, 1863, but the famed orator and invited keynote speaker, Mr. Edward Everett, was unable to make that date. The new date was November 19, and the inclusion of President Lincoln was definitely an afterthought. David Wills, the man most responsible for the creation of the Gettysburg National Cemetery, wrote to Lincoln on November 2. In his letter he requested: "It is the desire that after the oration, you, as Chief Executive of the nation, formally set apart these grounds to their sacred use by a few appropriate remarks." Lincoln agreed to attend the somber event.

There is no truth to the tale that Abraham Lincoln wrote the text of the Gettysburg Address on the back of an envelope as he took the train to the battlefield. He took nothing so important in such a cavalier manner. Instead, Lincoln worked on it for several days, handing off versions to his secretaries, John Hay and George Nicolay, for copying. The president had every intention of using this opportunity to "shore up the nation's resolve" for the continuance of the war, which showed no signs of abating.

The day before he was to speak, Lincoln, Nicolay, Hay, and Lincoln's political crony Ward Hill Lamon took the rails 80 miles to Gettysburg. The weather was unpleasantly rainy, and the president was not feeling well. The dignitaries who met the party at the train depot had to stand amid hundreds of wooden caskets. The reburial of the Union dead was only about one-third finished.

The next morning, David Wills and Lincoln took a tour on the battlefield on horseback, prompting a store

Lincoln's Gettysburg Address Memorial is dedicated to Lincoln's most famous speech, given at the battlefield on November 19, 1863, as a dedication of the Soldiers' National Cemetery. It is the only monument in the world dedicated to a speech and contains a bust of Abraham Lincoln flanked by two wings containing the text of the address and an explanation of the necessity for the Soldiers' Cemetery. The monument, not located at the actual spot where Lincoln spoke, is found in the south end of the National Cemetery, about 50 yards east of the Taneytown Gate. (cm)

clerk to observe that Lincoln appeared to be "the most peculiar-looking figure on horseback I had ever seen. . . . [I]t seemed to me that his feet almost touched the ground, but he was perfectly at ease."

Lincoln is not the man in the center of the photo wearing the stovepipe hat but the hatless man a quarter-inch to the left, stepping down from the platform. Lincoln spoke so briefly photographers were caught unprepared to snap a photo of the actual speech. (loc)

Camp Letterman was being packed up, and Dr. Henry Janes, who had managed the camp from the beginning, had been promised a chair on the speakers' platform. His staff, however, stood among the crowd. During the ceremony, Everett spoke for almost two hours before Ward Hill Lamon introduced Mr. Lincoln.

When one rereads the short text of the Gettysburg Address with the particulars of the battle in mind, the words are even more meaningful. Many of those standing in the crowd beneath the platform had met "on a great battlefield," and had struggled for weeks to honor "the brave men, living and dead," who had consecrated the ground upon which they stood. Those who saw for themselves the great suffering of the wounded, who tried to bury the dead with some sort of honor, who turned their entire town and the surrounding area into one huge hospital and morgue—for these people, Lincoln's words were a fitting tribute to the efforts not only of the soldiers and their officers, but to those who came afterward, to help wherever help was needed.

As Lincoln spoke, he looked out over the broken ground, ruined trees, and littered landscape that once had been a lovely little Pennsylvania town. So many men were dead, so many wounded in ways that would affect them for the rest of their lives . . . how to make sense of it all?

A statue of Lincoln on Baltimore Street in front of the Adams County Library, installed in November 2013 for the 150th anniversary of the Gettysburg Address, tries to capture the lofty rhetoric of the president's speech. The bronze statue weighs 800 pounds—much less weighty than Lincoln's 272 words. (cm)

In his unique way, Lincoln's majestic words repurposed the fallen soldiers. They were no longer just casualties on a long list; they were the "honored dead." Lincoln reminded his audience that the soldiers had made sacrifices to insure the permanence of the Union. For a generation whose parents remembered the Revolution, a democratic form of government was still a fragile thing, and worth protecting. "These dead shall not have died in vain," but did so for the noble causes of ending slavery in a "new birth of freedom," and to make certain that "government of the people, by the people, and for the people, shall not perish from the earth."

At Gettysburg's National Cemetery (Soldiers Cemetery)

The First Regimental Memorial— The 1st Minnesota Infantry:

This simple, marble flower urn, set on a large granite base, was the first regimental memorial at the Gettysburg battlefield. It was presented in November 1867 by living members of the regiment in honor of those who had "given their last full measure of devotion" in the battle. On July 2, the 300 men of the regiment made a desperate headlong charge to fill a gap in the Federal line even as Confederates surged toward it. Facing five-to-one odds, 170 of the Minnesotans fell as casualties. Their cemetery urn was planted with simple flowers and vines, and remains so, thanks to the efforts of Diane and Darryl Sannes, who adopted the small monument as a tribute to their native Minnesotans. Read this inspiring story here www.post.mnsun.com/2013/07/brooklyn-center-couple-adopts-first- monument-on-gettysburg-battlefield/.

The urn is located in the National Cemetery to the right of the Soldiers' National Monument facing Evergreen Cemetery.

The 1st Minnesota memorial honors the regiment, which suffered 82 percent casualties during the battle. (cm)

Kentucky Monument:

No Kentucky regiments fought for either side at the battle of Gettysburg, but Kentucky was the birthplace of both President Lincoln and Confederate President Jefferson Davis. "I hope to have God on my side, but I must have Kentucky," Lincoln said of the state, recognizing its political importance. A small Kentucky monument, situated in the National Cemetery east of the Soldier's National Monument, marks the spot where Lincoln delivered his Gettysburg Address.

"Kentucky honors her son, Abraham Lincoln, who delivered his immortal address at the site now marked by the Soldiers' Monument." (cm)

Sick of States Rights

CHAPTER ELEVEN
DECEMBER 25, 1863

In the mourning necklace of jet that is the United States National Cemetery system, the first bead strung was Chattanooga National Cemetery, located near Orchard Knob, Tennessee. Union Maj. Gen. George Henry Thomas established it on Christmas Day, 1863, with General Orders No. 296. Thomas first saw the geographic area during the assault of his troops that carried Missionary Ridge. After the Chattanooga campaign came to an end, he returned to the battlefield and appropriated 75 acres of land as a burial place for the lately fallen Union dead. Thomas personally saw to the burial of the Union soldiers who had died at Chattanooga. When a chaplain asked him if he wanted them separated by state as had been done at Gettysburg, Thompson is said to have replied, "No, no. Mix them all up. I am sick of state's rights."

Union chaplain Thomas V. Van Horne was placed in charge of the development of the cemetery. The chaplain had already designed the Marietta National Cemetery, established in 1866, as a final resting place for Union Maj. Gen. William T. Sherman's losses during the Atlanta campaign.

Van Horne soon hit a snag, though: at least one third of the plot chosen by Thomas could not be used for burials due to large rock outcroppings. To accommodate the geology of the Cumberland Plateau, he suggested an unusual design that incorporated the large rocks into the cemetery landscape. Flowering shrubs, evergreens, and other trees were planted to replace the portion of the

ABOVE: Maj. Gen. George Thomas, a native Virginian, stayed loyal to the Union when his home state seceded. (loc)

OPPOSITE: Lookout Mountain looms in the background over Chattanooga National Cemetery. (cm)

A monument to Andrews' Raiders—the perpetrators of what became known as "The Great Locomotive Chase"—was erected in 1891. The cemetery's Circle of Honor sits atop the hill in the background. (cm)

dense forest of oak trees that had been cut down as a part of the battleground. Each interment section consisted of a central site for a monument surrounded by plots for officers. The graves of enlisted personnel were arranged in concentric circles around them.

By 1870, more than 12,800 interments were completed in the cemetery, which had grown to 120 acres. The internments included men killed at the battles of Chickamauga, Missionary Ridge, and Lookout Mountain—including 1,798 sets of unknown remains from soldiers killed during the battle of Chickamauga. A final count at the time was 8,685 known and 4,189 unknown Civil War dead.

After World War I, the German government sought the location of any gravesites of German prisoners of war who had died while detained in the United States. The War Department found that 78 German POWs, the largest number buried anywhere, had been interred in Chattanooga, where there had been a detainment camp during the war. When the German government saw that their men had been buried with respect and dignity, they chose to leave them where they lay. A memorial, erected in 1935, still marks the spot.

Chattanooga National Cemetery is also designated as a Veteran's Administration cemetery, accepting casketed and cremated remains of veterans through 2015.

*   *   *

There are four unique monuments at Chattanooga National Cemetery with a connection to the Civil War. The first is a huge granite arch, the original entrance to the cemetery. It now stands near the artificial lake in the southwest corner of the grounds. It is one of five arches that served as formal entrances to national cemeteries found in the South. Three are managed by National Cemetery Association: Marietta, GA, built 1883; Chattanooga, TN, built ca.1880; and Nashville, TN, built ca.1870. These Roman-inspired structures are approximately 35 feet high with Doric columns, a pair of ornamental iron gates, and inscriptions above. The two other memorial arches are found at Arlington National Cemetery, built in 1879, and Vicksburg National Cemetery, ca. 1880—properties managed by the Department of Defense and National Park Service, respectively.

Tabler Vineyard's family owned the farm—Viniard farm—where the battle of Chickamauga erupted in September 1863. The fight inspired Tabler to join the 1st Georgia Infantry—a guerilla force for the Federal army. His eldest son, James, joined the Confederate army. Tabler survived until August of 1864, when he died of diarrhea. James, meanwhile, died of smallpox in 1865 while a captive in a Federal prison in Alton, Illinois. (cm)

On a small hill at the Circle of Honor in the center of the cemetery, four cannon are set into concrete bases with their muzzles facing the sky. Between the arch and the cannon is a memorial to each branch of the service. In 1868, the IV Army Corps erected a tall, white granite obelisk to honor their fallen comrades. It can be found between Sections C and F.

A most unusual addition to this collection of tributes is the Andrews' Raiders Monument (sometimes called the "Ohio Monument"), dedicated to Union spy James J. Andrews and 24 of his men, who were responsible for the "Great Locomotive Chase." Andrews and his men maneuvered deep into Confederate territory to destroy railroads and communication lines. On April 12, 1862, they hijacked a wood-burning locomotive known as *The General* at Marietta, Georgia.

The raiders rode from the station at Big Shanty (now Kennesaw), Georgia, tearing up rails along the way. The upset conductor, William Allen Fuller, and two other men gave chase, commandeering others trains to overcome the track damage. Eighty miles later, he caught up with *The General* and the Union men in Ringold, Georgia. Andrews and his men jumped from the engine and scattered into the forest, but within two weeks, Andrews and his men were captured.

The Confederates charged Andrews and seven others with "acts of unlawful belligerency," tried them in Chattanooga courts, and found them guilty. They were hung and buried without ceremony in unmarked graves. Six of the men were later awarded the Medal of Honor by Secretary of War Edwin M. Stanton, and were reinterred in Chattanooga National Cemetery. James Andrews did not receive the Medal of Honor; his status as a civilian made him ineligible. The monument, which includes the graves of those who took part in the Great Locomotive Chase and a granite pedestal topped with a bronze, scaled-down version of *The General* itself, is in section H of the Chattanooga National Cemetery.

To find out more about this site, check their web page at www.nps.gov/nr/travel/national_cemeteries/tennessee/Chattanooga_National_Cemetery.html.

At Chattanooga's Confederate Cemeteries

The Chattanooga Area Relic & Historical Association (CARHA) owns and maintains Silverdale. Visit the Chattanooga Area Relic & Historical Association's website at www.carha.org. (mg)

Silverdale Confederate cemetery, found at 7710 Lee Highway, Chattanooga, Tennessee, is a well-kept jewel. and a continuation of the labor of love begun by the Ladies Memorial Associations immediately after the war—to locate and reinter all remains of Confederate soldiers wherever possible.

Initially, the cemetery was made up of a plot of land containing 155 Confederate soldiers of the Army of the Tennessee who died while hospitalized during the mobilization of Confederate Gen. Braxton Bragg's Kentucky campaign of September-October 1862. The hospital marked the individual graves with wooden markers indicating name, rank, and organization. Over time, the wooden markers deteriorated and most of the graves lost their identification. When the remains were reinterred, they occupied a mass grave.

The valiant efforts of CARHA, a group of private citizens, have restored this memorial plot of land to almost pristine beauty and dignity. Their work to identify individual soldiers is ongoing, and several have been identified. The cemetery has been referred to as "a step back in time, a small gem" and "a beautiful place to ponder your soul."

Another interesting cemetery in the area is the Chattanooga Confederate Cemetery. Just as the Silverdale Confederate Cemetery holds the remains of the men who died at the Wither's Hospital at Tyner's Station, so this cemetery holds the remains of those who died in the chain of small Confederate hospitals opened by Dr. Samuel H. Stout to care for Confederate General Braxton Bragg's Army of the Tennessee.

In July of 1863, Bragg commanded his soldiers to

begin evacuating the Chattanooga area to escape the predations of Union Maj. Gen. William Rosecrans and his Army of the Cumberland. Originally, Dr. Stout buried those who had died in his hospitals on a plot of land beside the Tennessee River near the current location of the Manker Patten Tennis Club. Rain and flooding threatened the area regularly, destroying the wooden headboards and disinterring a corpse upon occasion. When it was not raining, the fields were part pasture and part baseball diamond.

The cemetery was moved the first time in 1867. $750 was raised to purchase the northern portion of the current site, and bones were boxed for reinterment. By the 1880s, the cemetery was managed with the cooperation of the city of Chattanooga. During the work of creating the Chickamauga and Chattanooga cemeteries, more bodies were discovered. When they could not be identified, they ended up in the Chattanooga Confederate Cemetery. In 1901, the United Confederate Veterans and the Daughters of the Confederacy joined forces in support of the burial ground. More land was added when Francis M. Gardenshire deeded the southern end of the current plot to the groups for one dollar. His only proviso was that the land only be used for a Confederate Cemetery.

The centerpiece of the Confederate cemetery is the large Memorial Obelisk, designed by G. C. Conner. It was dedicated on May 10, 1877. This occasion was the first in Chattanooga in which veterans of both armies came together with local citizens to exchange fraternal well wishes and extend the hand of friendship to one another. (gb/pp)

Although the cemetery has good years and bad, it was completely restored in 1992 and rededicated at a large ceremony three years later. In 2000, the last burial in the cemetery involved the remains of a soldier found during the excavation for a swimming pool on Missionary Ridge. It is not known whether that particular soldier wore the blue or the gray, but in the tradition begun when bodies found during the work on the Chickamauga and Chattanooga National Cemetery were buried in the Confederate Cemetery, so this soldier found his final rest there as well.

One grave does hold a known Union soldier. Sergeant Edward J. Wentworth of the 19th Michigan Infantry was on his way to a military prison when he was offloaded in Chattanooga. His condition was near death. In April 1863, Wentworth finally succumbed to his injuries in the Academy Hospital despite the care of Confederate doctors and nurses. He now rests peacefully with his former foes.

A lone Confederate grave remains on the Chickamauga battlefield itself: Pvt. John Ingraham, a local man killed during the battle and buried there by friends to keep him close to home. (cm)

The Chattanooga Confederate Cemetery is located adjacent to the grounds of the University of Tennessee at Chattanooga. It lies between the Citizens Cemetery and the Mizpah Cemetery and is well cared-for. Most of the graves are unmarked, and there are many Unknowns, including 2500 buried in one mass grave.

Ending the Eternal Patrol

CHAPTER TEWLVE

FEBRUARY 17, 1864

Seaman Robert F. Flemming saw it first, and perhaps he saw it last, as well. At about 8:40 p.m., the young black man had just come for his watch on the *U.S.S. Housatonic.* The winter night was dark and cold, bitterly cold, on February 17, 1864. Charleston Harbor had become a forbidding place, filled with Union warships guarding its namesake southern city of Charleston, South Carolina. The *Housatonic* looked daily at war-torn Fort Sumter, where the Civil War had started in 1861. Sumter could be seen that night, as well, a low, dark line in the shimmering moonlight of the glassy harbor.

As Flemming looked across the water, he noticed . . . something. A log? There were rumors of a Confederate "fish-ship," being developed—a submarine of some sort. . . . Perhaps. . . .

Seaman Flemming hesitated for only a few seconds before he decided to deliver his findings to Acting Master's Mate Lewis A. Cornthwait. Cornthwait questioned Flemming, who replied, "It's not a log, sir. It's not floating with the tide like a log would. It's moving across the tide."

John Crosby, the Acting Master of the *Housatonic,* believed Flemming's report concerning the *log that was not a log.*

By 8:50, the *log* had delivered its 90-pound load of explosives. The mighty Union sailing vessel was sinking, a huge hole punched into her starboard quarter, forcing her to lurch heavily to port. Most of the crew had been in their bunks when the left side of the ship disappeared

ABOVE: *The Hunley* **crew was to signal for rescue with a blue light.** (cm)

OPPOSITE: A recreation of the *The Hunley's* **interior lets visitors to the Hunley Center experience for themselves what it was like to sit in a cramped, claustrophobic metal death tube.** (cm)

into the water, tossing them into the cold, dark ocean. Flemming, who clung to the foremast, was among the survivors. He hung there almost an hour, waiting for rescue from the nearby *Canandaigua*.

A cut-away model on display at the Hunley Center shows the men at work on the crank-shaft that powered the sub.
(cm)

As he looked out over the waters of Charleston Harbor, Flemming saw a small flash of light. He instantly recognized it as a "blue light," not blue in color any more by that time, but a pyrotechnical signal from one ship to another to indicate "Mission Accomplished." It was at this point that Union Seaman Robert Flemming realized the impossible had happened: an undersea vessel had sunk a large, seagoing ship.

Flemming was not the only person to see the flash of light. Confederate soldiers, rubbing their cold hands together and blowing into them as they waited on the shore, saw it, too. It was the agreed-upon signal from the eight-man crew of the tiny "fish boat," the submarine *H. L. Hunley*, that their mission had indeed been accomplished. The men on shore quickly lit their brands and torched the large pile of driftwood and debris to create a bonfire large enough to be seen a dozen miles out to sea. No one really knew what had happened—and no one would know for another 131 years.

*   *   *

February 18, 1864, was a snowy day in Charleston. The ashes of the now-dead bonfire blew around, mixing in the light snow flurries. Lieutenant Colonel O. M. Dantzler wondered where Lt. George E. Dixon, commander of the *Hunley* was. No one knew if a Union ship had been sunk, as the short encounter occurred four miles from the shore.

But when no word had been heard from the *Hunley* by the 19th, Dantzler was pretty sure the little black submarine and its eight-man crew was not coming home. He sadly wrote to Confederate general P. G. T. Beauregard, now commander of Charleston's coastal defenses: "I have the honor to report that the torpedo-boat stationed at this point went out on the night of the 17th instant and has not returned."

The *Hunley* was lost at sea and considered to be on *eternal patrol*, a sad euphemism for submarines that never return to shore.

*   *   *

According to the Naval History & Heritage Command, at least 4,101 naval casualties were incurred during the Civil War. 2260 of these men died outright. However, these numbers represent Union Navy and Marine losses only. There is practically no information on Confederate statistics because the South had to create a navy from scratch. Confederate Secretary of the Navy Stephen Mallory was an admiralty lawyer before he became a U. S. senator from Florida and had no naval experience at all. By February 1861, only fourteen ships in the nascent Rebel sea force were even considered seaworthy. The South had to rely on technical innovations such as ironclads, naval mines, and a tiny group of torpedo boats—or submarines—to protect their coastline.

Trauma medicine during a battle at sea combined the jangled nerves of being under fire with the claustrophobia of a confined space and the motion of waves. (mg)

Battles at sea leave scars just as land battles do, albeit of a different kind. Naval weaponry damaged ships and men alike, sometimes requiring a time out of service for both. If a battle was conducted far from shore, those who were rescued or survived brought names and information about their fellow sailors to land with them and turned the information over to their superiors. Bodies were given a burial at sea or, if there was no body to bury, their names were mentioned in a brief ceremony. Many simply went down with their ships to lie among the wreckage

A chaplain conducts an on-board service over a flag-draped coffin before the body is consigned to the sea. (ncwcm)

at the bottom of the ocean. Just as the Civil War dead on land were often unknown, so could be deceased sailors and marines.

As time passed, and technology, science, and forensics improved, the possibilities grew greater that ships sunk during the Civil War might be raised and their crews identified and more properly buried. The story of the *Hunley* is one such example of how her aftermath was postponed more than a hundred years.

Since no one ever saw the *Hunley* again after February

A replica of *The Hunley* sits along Meeting Street in Charleston outside the Charleston Museum. The harpoon that held the torpedo was mounted on the top of the replica, which was made before the real sub was recovered. Archeological work on the sub revealed that the harpoon was actually mounted on *The Hunley*'s bottom. (cm)

17, 1864, no one knew exactly what had happened to her. Had the explosion of the *Housatonic* been so strong that it had sunk the fragile little submersible as well? This was the most reasonable of the explanations that floated around for many years, although every so often someone would report having seen George Dixon, captain of the *Hunley*, at a bar or a hotel. These sightings were never confirmed. All anyone knew was that the letters Dixon wrote to his young fiancé, Queenie Bennett, stopped coming, leaving another broken heart on the Confederate home front. A year later, Charleston fell to the Union, and in April 1865, the Civil War ended.

The tiny Confederate submarine *H. L. Hunley* had claimed thirteen lives during her short existence. The undersea vessel had been privately constructed in Mobile, Alabama, based on the plans of marine engineer Horace Lawson Hunley. She was constructed from a 40-foot-long cylindrical iron steam boiler, with a tapered bow and stern. After successful tests on the Mobile River, the submarine was transported to Charleston in August 1863. It was hoped by the Confederate navy that she could be a secret weapon for breaking the powerful Union blockade.

Shortly after testing began in Charleston Harbor, five of the *Hunley's* nine crewmembers drowned when a ship's officer accidentally caused the vessel to dive while the hatches were still open. The submarine was salvaged, but less than two months later, a second training accident killed the eight-member crew, including the craft's designer, H. L. Hunley himself.

Once again, the submarine was pulled to the surface, and even though he knew her tragic history, Lt. George Dixon agreed to take command of the vessel in November 1863. He raised a crew of seven volunteers. As Dixon led

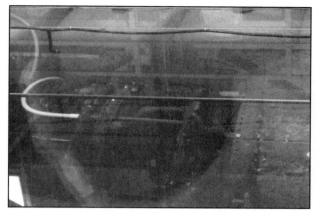

The salvaged hulk of *The Hunley* has undergone years of meticulous conservation, including chemical baths to remove a century and a half of rust and ocean crust. Visitors to the Hunley Center can see the sub on display and learn about the techniques employed to restore and conserve it. (cm)

his men in the attack on *Housatonic*, he carried with him his good luck charm, a bent gold coin that had saved his life by slowing a bullet that had wounded him two years before at the battle of Shiloh. Although Beauregard had instructed Dixon to keep the boat on the surface during any attacks, given *Hunley's* previous accidents, most of the submarine still remained below the water line as it moved close to the *Housatonic*.

Seven Confederate sailors inside the primitive submarine turned a hand crank that powered the propeller as Dixon steered his fragile craft toward the 1,240-ton sloop-of-war. Even if they had not been bearing down on a mighty warship, the eight men were already undertaking a dangerous mission simply by being inside a craft that had already claimed the lives of thirteen men, including its inventor, during training exercises.

After being spotted, the captain and crew of the *Housatonic* fired their rifles and shotguns in a futile attempt to halt the approaching vessel, but the bullets merely bounced off the *Hunley's* armor. A spar torpedo mounted at the end of a 16-foot rod that protruded from the submarine's bow tore into the *Housatonic's* starboard quarter near its powder magazine—and then the rebel torpedo, laden with 135 pounds of gunpowder, exploded.

The *Housatonic* took on water immediately, and within minutes it was a loss, the first warship to have ever been sunk by a submarine, but the *Hunley* herself also slipped to the bottom of Charleston Harbor.

In 1995, the submarine was located beneath sand and shells by novelist Clive Cussler's National Underwater and Marine Agency. Five years later, the well-preserved wreck of the *Hunley*, with her eight-member crew still at their stations and Dixon still with his lucky coin, was raised from its murky grave and brought to the Warren Lasch Conservation Center in North Charleston. It was placed

According to legend, *Hunley* commander Lt. George Dixon kept in his pocket a gold coin given to him by his sweetheart, Queenie Bennett of Mobile, Alabama. At the battle of Shiloh, the coin saved Dixon from a point-blank shot: the coin stopped the bullet, which bent the coin. Afterwards, Dixon inscribed "My life preserver" on the coin's back side. When *The Hunley* was salvaged, scientists found the gold coin next to Dixon's remains. (cm)

in a 90,000-gallon freshwater conservation tank where slowly and carefully, one piece at a time, working from x-rays of the ship's interior, her crew was finally removed.

Much of the mystery of the *Hunley* involves these

eight men: only one was believed to have had children, and there are no known photographs of any of the eight, including her captain, Lt. George Dixon. They ranged in age from their late teens to their mid-40s, and some had teeth that bore the hallmarks of prolific pipe smoking. Two are known only by their last names.

Modern forensics have allowed scientists to reconstruct the faces of *The Hunely*'s crew. (cm)

In 2004, after a parade through the city, the crew members of *The Hunley* were laid to rest with full military honors in Magnolia Cemetery. (ds)

Every bit of 21st century forensics continues to be used to examine the remains of the *Hunley* herself, and the men who worked the boat. Forensic artist Sharon Long and physical anthropologist Dr. Douglas Owsley joined talents under the auspices of the Friends of the *Hunley* to do facial reconstructions of the crewmembers. Genealogy researcher Linda Abrams has attempted to untangle the lives of the crew, often meeting with seemingly insurmountable obstacles. Only two of the eight were from a Confederate state. One of those had recently served

in the U. S. Navy before joining the Southern war effort. Four were born in Europe and had recently immigrated to America. Five of them were recruited from the *C. S. S. Indian Chief*, which was stationed in Charleston Harbor.

We now know their names, or at least their last names: James Wicks, Frank Collins, Joseph Ridgaway, Arnold Becker, J. F. Carlson, Lumpkin, and Miller. Lieutenant George Dixon commanded them, and shared their fate. All eight skeletonized remains were found still at their stations, some with their bony fingers still on the crank.

The crew of the *Hunley* was given a proper burial in 2004 at Magnolia Cemetery in Charleston. They lie with other members of her former crews: Horace Lawson Hunley, who designed the "fish boat," Thomas Parks, who built her, and her first captain, Charles L. Sprague—*Hunley* casualties all.

The "Hunley Center": Clemson University's Warren Lasch Conservation Lab, located at 1250 Supply Street, North Charleston, South Carolina. More information can be found through the Friends of the Hunley at www.hunley.org. (cm)

The crews of the *Hunley* and the *Housatonic* were also remembered on February 17, 2001, in a memorial ceremony on Sullivan's Island, at the entrance to Charleston Harbor. On the "137th anniversary of their sacrifice," more than three hundred people gathered for a church service followed by a short walk ending at Breach Inlet at the exact hour the little sub would have departed. Reenactors representing both the North and the South fired a twenty-one-gun salute to honor the departed, and women in full mourning threw roses into the water. The silent, respectful thoughts and prayers of those who attended the memorial seem appropriate stand-is for the loved ones of long ago.

Sometimes an aftermath is a long time coming.

A Death-like Stillness Prevails

CHAPTER THIRTEEN

SPRING 1864

Mrs. Mary Custis Lee had begun her early-May morning in 1861 as she usually did, with a thin porcelain teacup of black chicory-flavored coffee. She sat at the window in her bedroom, which overlooked the Arlington flower garden. The garden had always brought her such joy, even when ravaged by the pet rabbits her children loved in earlier days. It was designed by English architect George Hadfield and planted by her grandfather, George Washington Parke Custis. The garden was far from formal. It ran riot with flowers grown from clippings Mary had brought from other family estates or given to her as gifts from visitors. It was her place of peace, and one of the features she was most proud of at her ancestral estate. Why, in 1824 the Marquis de Lafayette himself had complimented its fragrance during his visit to America. Sitting high atop the heights that overlooked Washington, on the far side of the Potomac River, Arlington House offered one of the most splendid views in Northern Virginia.

Mary had just taken another sip of coffee when her cousin, young Lt. Orton W. Williams, burst in upon her solitude. Despite his Southern sympathies, Williams's resignation from Union Gen. Winfield Scott's staff had not yet been accepted. "You must pack up all you value immediately and send it off," Williams warned her. Mary's husband, Robert E. Lee, had resigned his army commission and left on April 24 to travel to Richmond, where he had been asked to command Virginia's military forces. He, too, had written that she should begin moving

ABOVE: Mary Custis's family built Arlington in the early 1800s. Robert E. Lee, a lieutenant in the U.S. Army, married Mary in the home in 1831. (loc)

OPPOSITE: With President John F. Kennedy's eternal flame burning in the foreground, Robert E. Lee's former home, Arlington House, stands as another enduring tribute. (cm)

Quartermaster General Montgomery Meigs was arguably the second-most powerful man in the entire United States Army because of the control he wielded over logistics and supplies. (loc)

the valuables and important Revolutionary War artifacts of Arlington House. She had begun packing, but now, apparently, timing was essential. Just before her departure, Mary wrote to General Scott, "Were it not that I would not add one more feather to his [Robert's] load of care, nothing would induce me to abandon my home."

She also wrote sadly to her husband, "I never saw the country more beautiful, perfectly radiant. The yellow jasmine in full bloom and perfuming the air; but a death-like stillness prevails everywhere."

Arlington House not only offered a lovely view of northern Virginia, it offered an equally commanding view of Washington, D.C. In order to protect the Union capital from the high ground on the south bank of the Potomac, the city of Alexandria, as well as the mansion, were to be put under military occupation as soon as the citizens of Virginia ratified their ordinance of secession. By the time the Federal army was sitting in the parlor wing of the Arlington House on May 23-24, Mary's allegiance to the Southern Confederacy was sealed. There was no going back, unless it was to once again occupy her beloved home.

Mrs. Lee was not the only person who felt a proprietary interest in the estate, however.

* * *

Brigadier General Montgomery Meigs, a West Point graduate of the class of 1836, was, in the words of James G. Blaine, "one of the ablest graduates of the Military Academy," and by the end of the Civil War, second in importance to the Union army only to General in Chief Ulysses S. Grant.

General Meigs was also a serious holder of grudges.

Meigs had, earlier in his career, served under Robert E. Lee in the Engineering Corps, but when Colonel Lee resigned his commission in the United States Army to join the Confederacy, Meigs was angered and appalled. In a letter to his father, Meigs wrote that Lee, Joseph Johnston, and Jefferson Davis "should be put formally out of the way if possible by sentence of death . . . executed if caught." As the war progressed, Meigs's attitude never got any better, even though Joseph E. Johnston's resignation from the army had opened up the slot into which Meigs was inserted—Quartermaster General for the Federal army. In fact, over time, Meigs grew even more hard-hearted toward the Confederates, whom he considered

Brig. Gen. Irvin McDowell (fifth from the right) stands with his staff on the front steps of Arlington. (loc)

traitors. "No man who ever took the oath to support the Constitution as an officer of our Army or Navy . . . should escape without the loss of all his goods & civil rights & expatriation," he fumed.

On May 24, 1861, Federal troops took possession of the small town of Alexandria. This included Mrs. Lee's house. Within a few days, Brig. Gen. Irvin McDowell made her front lawn his headquarters, gallantly declining to occupy Mary's white Hellenic mansion.

But McDowell would not remain in command for long, replaced following the loss at Manassas by Maj. Gen. George McClellan. While McClellan used Washington as his headquarters, the land around Arlington House, as well as the house itself, became trampled and showed signs of hard use because of the enlistees converging on the capital to fill the ranks of the army. The lovely old oaks surrounding the home disappeared one by one as the winter months of 1861-62 approached and firewood became necessary.

"Our old home, if not destroyed, will be difficult ever to be recognized," Robert E. Lee wrote to his wife. Resigned to the inevitable, he tried to convince Mary to accept the loss of Arlington House. Mrs. Lee remained upset, complaining passionately to all within earshot. Nevertheless, there was little she could do from her refugee home at Ravensworth Plantation, in Fairfax County, with the war going on around her, and no end in sight.

*   *   *

A year later, a legal technicality enabled the federal government to purchase the Custis-Lee home and the land surrounding it for $26,800—much less than its assessed value. The aim of the government purchase was to use the property for "Government use, for war, military, charitable and educational purposes."

By the spring of 1864, Washington, D.C.'s temporary hospitals were overflowing with sick and dying soldiers, who were quickly filling up already-overcrowded local cemeteries. General Lee and Union commander General Grant had begun their blistering Overland Campaign, exchanging blows from the Wilderness to Petersburg.

Montgomery Meigs already held a grudge against Robert E. Lee because of Lee's defection from the army, but in the fall of 1864, Meigs' grudge took on an entirely personal dimension. His 22-year-old son, Lt. John Rogers Meigs (top), was killed on Oct. 3, 1864, during a scouting expedition in the Shenandoah Valley. The young Meigs was buried beneath a tomb topped by a recumbent bronze statue (above). Because the elder Meigs held Lee personally accountable, he buried young John within close sight of Lee's house. (loc)(cm)

The fighting produced some 84,000 casualties in just over a month. Quartermaster General Meigs cast about for new graveyards to accommodate the rising tide of bodies. His keen eye spied Arlington and on June 15, 1864, he wrote to Secretary of War Edwin Stanton:

> *I have visited and inspected the grounds now used as a Cemetery upon the Arlington Estate. I recommend that interments in this ground be discontinued and that the land surrounding the Arlington Mansion, now understood to be the property of the United States, be appropriated as a National Cemetery, to be properly enclosed, laid out, and carefully preserved for that purpose, and that the bodies recently interred be removed to the National Cemetery thus to be established. The grounds about the Mansion are admirably adapted for such a use.*

Stanton personally endorsed Meigs's recommendation the next day. The *Washington Morning Chronicle* heralded the idea: "This and the Freedman's Village are righteous uses of the estate of the Rebel General Lee."

Meigs had a moment of upset when he toured his new cemetery, however. Graves were being dug, but they were placed far from the Arlington mansion. He quickly ascertained the real issue—none of the Union officers stationed at the house wished to be *that* close to the buried dead, so the burial details were ordered to begin digging in the Lower Cemetery where there were already graves. Almost instantly, the complaining officers lost their mansion headquarters to a more compliant military chaplain and his staff. The order was given: *I want these men buried so close to the house that they* [the Lee family] *can never live there again.*

Mary Lee's rose garden was encircled with the graves of Federal officers. At the end of her garden. Meigs excavated a huge, circular pit. Its pie-shaped pieces were

The Tomb of the Unknown Civil War Soldiers reads: "Beneath this stone repose the bones of two thousand one hundred and eleven unknown soldiers gathered after the war from the fields of Bull Run, and the route to the Rappahannock, their remains could not be identified. But their names and deaths are recorded in the archives of their country, and its grateful citizens honor them as of their noble army of martyrs." (cm)

filled with the bones and skulls of 2,111 Union dead who were unidentified. It was topped with a sarcophagus erected in their honor.

As a final, immensely sad, and personal gesture of retribution, Meigs buried the remains of his 22-year-old "noble, precious son," Lt. John Rodgers Meigs, on the Arlington property. Young Lieutenant Meigs was shot on October 3, 1864, as he scouted the Shenandoah Valley for Gen. Phil Sheridan. Initially Meigs's son was buried with full honors in a private cemetery in Georgetown, with President Lincoln, Secretary Stanton, and other Washington dignitaries at the services. However, as soon as it was certain that the Federal government would control the area around Arlington, Meigs moved his son's remains, interring him within site of the mansion: Row 1, Section 1.

Meigs grew even more vitriolic toward the South as the war continued. When Lee finally surrendered to Grant on April 9, 1865, Meigs was more angry and bitter than ever. Although he had created a lasting memorial to the Union dead, he could not rest peacefully. "The rebels are all murderers of my son and the sons of thousands," he said. "Justice seems not satisfied if they escape judicial trial and execution."

Mrs. Lee desperately wanted her home back, but it was obvious that Arlington had become hallowed ground. It was no longer a burial place for unknown soldiers; it had become a shrine for the "patriot graves" of the "sacred dead."

Meigs went on to further develop the cemetery into what it is today. He designed and built the wisteria-draped amphitheater for ceremonies within the cemetery grounds, which was dedicated in 1874. All during the 1870s, he designed the plantings for the borders of the garden, personally gave consent to the tombstones and monuments of the officers' section, and oversaw

Philip Kearny "gave his left arm at Churubusco, Mexico, August 14, 1847, and his life at Chantilly, Virginia, September 1, 1862," his monument reads. Originally buried in New York, Kearny's body was moved to Arlington in 1912. (cm)

Secretary of War Robert Todd Lincoln, the only surviving son of the president, negotiated final sale of the Arlington property to the federal government. He was buried in Arlington following his death in 1926 at age 82. (CM)

construction of the red marble McClellan arch that one passes today to enter the cemetery grounds. It was finally finished in 1879. Atop the gate on the eastern side are the words from Theodore O'Hara's poem, "The Bivouac of the Dead."

On fame's eternal camping ground
Their silent tents are spread,
And Glory guards, with solemn round,
The bivouac of the dead.

On the western side of the gate, the poem continues.

Rest on, embalmed and sainted dead!
Dear as the blood ye gave;
No impious footstep here shall tread
The herbage of your grave.

By December, 1882, the federal government agreed to pay $150,000 for Arlington House. The exchange of money for the property deed took place on March 31, 1883, and Robert Todd Lincoln, then Secretary of War and son of President Abraham Lincoln, accepted the title from Custis Lee, son of Robert E. Lee.

Meigs went on to produce many well-known Washington buildings, including the National Building Museum (formerly the Old Pension Building), both wings of the U.S. Capitol Building as well as its dome, the Union Arch, and the Washington Aqueduct. Meigs often visited "his" cemetery, and oversaw the burial of his family at Arlington, including his wife, father, and numerous in-laws, as well as his son, John. On a chilly January day in 1892, Gen. Montgomery Meigs made his last trip to Arlington Cemetery. Funeral drums played their muffled cadence, the smoke from the rifled salute hung in the heavy winter air, and the bugler played "Taps" as the general was buried in the spectacular memorial cemetery he created.

At Arlington Nationale Cemetery

Visiting Arlington National Cemetery is a serious business. There are many rules that concern proper dress and behavior that have been codified in the Federal Regulations, Title 32: National Defense, Part 553—Army National Cemeteries. This document may be found on the cemetery's website: www.arlingtoncemetery.mil.

Please check the website listed prior to any visit. The cemetery is open 365 days a year, but quite often an unscheduled event interrupts its schedule. In general, visitors cannot use the site to picnic, play, walk dogs, or wear revealing clothing. It is a cemetery, after all. That being said, it is a lovely and welcoming place.

The website for Arlington includes an interactive PDF file map that shows many of the interesting places within the grounds of the site itself. No longer just a Civil War cemetery, service members from World Wars I and II are buried there, as well as Korea, Vietnam, and the Middle East. There is a memorial to Pan Am Flight 103, one to the astronauts who lost their lives in both the *Challenger* and the *Columbia* missions, and a group burial for the Pentagon victims of the 9/11 attacks.

Of Civil War interest is the Confederate Memorial, in the eastern part of the site along McPherson Drive. It is surrounded by Jackson Circle and contains the remains of Confederate soldiers who had been buried in other places within the cemetery as well as those who were buried at the Soldiers' Home in Washington, and the National Cemetery at Alexandria, Virginia. They were collected and reinterred at the memorial, erected by the United Daughters of the Confederacy on June 4, 1914. The 482 people buried at the Confederate Memorial include 46 officers, 361 enlisted men, 58 wives, 15 civilians, and 12 unknowns. They are buried in concentric circles surrounding the main monument, and the pointed tops of the marble headstones distinguish their graves. The story is told that this shape was chosen for two reasons: to make Confederate markers different from Union markers, and to "keep the Yankees from sitting on them."

Another topic of interest is the Tomb of the Unknowns. The one most people are familiar with is at the Memorial Amphitheater between Memorial and Roosevelt Drives. This is the one shown on television every Memorial Day when the president of the United States takes part in the wreath-laying ceremony. This is NOT the one built by Montgomery Meigs, however. The grave of the Civil War Unknowns is north of the Memorial Amphitheater, and on the grounds of the Arlington House. It and the original Memorial Section are south and a bit west of the Kennedy Memorials, and to the right off Sherman Drive.

Sculptor Moses Ezekiel, who is buried at the foot of his Confederate Memorial, was a graduate of the Virginia Military Institute and had fought at the battle of New Market in May 1864. As an internationally renowned artist, Ezekiel went on to sculpt VMI's memorial to the cadets killed at New Market, *Virginia Mourning Her Dead*, as well as the statue of Stonewall Jackson that stands at the head of the campus's parade ground. (cm)

Notable Civil War Burials at Arlington National Cemetery

compiled by Chris Mackowski and Daniel T. Davis

Section 1

Alexander, Augusta—First black physician in the U.S. army; leader of the Freedmen's hospital in Washington, D.C.; regimental surgeon for the 7th U.S.C.T.; first black professor of medicine in the U.S. (Grave 124)

Auger, Christopher—Division commander in the Army of the Gulf; Commander of the XXII Corps (Grave 63)

Ayres, Romeyn—Brigade and division commander of the U.S. Regulars in the Army of the Potomac (Grave 12)

Baird, Absalom—Division commander in the Army of the Cumberland's XIV Corps; Medal of Honor recipient (Grave 55)

Benet, Stephen Vincent—Father of the American poet who wrote "John Brown's Body" (Grave 154)

Bliss, Zenas—Brigade commander in the Army of the Potomac's IX Corps; Medal of Honor recipient (Grave 8-B)

Doubleday, Abner—Division commander in I Corps of Army of the Potomac; formerly credited with being the inventor of baseball (Grave 61)

Hazen, William B.—Defended "Hell's Half-Acre" at Stones River; division commander in the Army of the Tennessee (Grave 15)

Hopkins, Juliet—"Florence Nightingale of the South" (Grave 12)

Krzyzanowski, Wladimir—Polish nobleman who served as a brigadier general in the Army of the Potomac (Grave 832)

Marthon, Joseph—Lt. Commander in the Navy; served with Farragut during battle of Mobile Bay (Grave 103-A)

Montgomery, Meigs—Quartermaster General of the United States Army (Grave 1)

Ord, Edward—Commander of the Army of the James (Grave 982)

Paul, Gabriel—Brigadier general who began service in Mexico; blinded at Gettysburg on July 1 (Grave 16)

Powell, John Wesley—Officer in Western armies; first American explorer of the Grand Canyon (Grave 408)

Randolph, Wallace Fitz—Escapee from Libby Prison; first Chief of U.S. Artillery (Grave 132)

Wheaton, Frank—Brigade commander in the Army of the Potomac's VI Corps (Grave 131-A)

Willcox, Orlando—Division commander in the IX Corps of the Army of the Potomac (Grave 18)

Section 2

Berdan, Hiram—Inventor of the Berdan rifle and commander of the United States Volunteer Sharpshooters (Grave 979)

Brooke, John Rutter—brigade commander in the Army of the Potomac's II Corps (Grave 1031)

Clem, John Lincoln—Drummer boy for the 22nd Michigan; youngest noncommissioned officer (age 12) in army history (Grave 992)

Crook, George—Commander of the Army of West Virginia (Grave 974)

Gibbon, John—Division commander in II Corps of the Army of the Potomac; XXIV Corps commander of the Army of the James (Grave 986)

Henry, Guy—Civil War colonel; Medal of Honor recipient (Grave 990)

Kautz, August—Union cavalry commander, served in the Eastern and Western armies (Grave 992)

Kearny, Philip—Division commander in the Army of the Potomac; killed at the battle of Chantilly (Grave S-8)

McArthur, Arthur—Served in the Army of the Cumberland; Medal of Honor recipient; ather of Gen. Douglas McArthur (Grave 879

McMahon, Martin—Chief of Staff of Army of the Potomac's VI Corps; Medal of Honor recipient (Grave 1101)

McClellan, George B.—Commander of the Army of the Potomac; "The Young Napoleon"; 1864 Democratic candidate for president (Grave 3394)

Mower, Joseph—Commander in the Western armies; a.k.a. "The Swamp Lizard"(Grave 1041)

Porter, David Dixon—Acclaimed Naval hero (Grave S-5)

Rawlins, John—U.S. Grant's chief of staff during the war; Secretary of War (Grave 1007)

Schofield, John—Commander of the Army of the Ohio; Interim Secretary of War; Commanding General of the Army; Medal of Honor recipient (Grave 1108)

Sheridan, Phillip—division commander in the Army of the Cumberland; cavalry chief for the Army of the Potomac; General in Chief of the Army; self-promoter (Grave S-1)

Spear, Ellis—Colonel in the 20th Maine; later brevetted major general (Grave 4699)

Sturgis, Samuel—division commander in Army of the Potomac's IX Corps; cavalry commander in Western Theater; famously said "I don't care for John Pope one pinch of owl dung." (Grave 1044)

Wheeler, Joseph—Confederate cavalry commander in Western Theater; called into Federal service during Spanish-American and Philippine-American wars (Grave 1089)

Wint, Theodore—Cavalry private who rose to rank of brigadier general after war; large grave commissioned as a public art project by Commonwealth of PA (Grave 846-847)

Wright, Horatio—VI Corps commander in Army of the Potomac (Grave S-4)

Section 3

Belknap, William Worth—Major general under Sherman; Secretary of War under Grant (Grave 2231)

Benteen, Frederick—Cavalry officer with 10th Missouri; played controversial role in Little Big Horn massacre (Grave 1351SS)

Letterman, Jonathan—Chief Medical Office of the Army of the Potomac; "Father of Battlefield Medicine" (Grave 1869)

Miles, Nelson—Division commander in Army of the Potomac's II Corps; Medal of Honor recipient; General in Chief of the Army (Grave 1873)

Ream, Vinnie (Hoxie)—Sculptor of Abraham Lincoln; grave marked with replica of her sculpture, *Sappho* (Grave 1876)

Rice, Edmund—Medal of Honor recipient; grave shows a replica of the MoH (Grave 1875)

Roscrans, William Stark—commander of the Army of the Cumberland (Grave 1862)

Sickles, Daniel—III Corps commander in Army of the Potomac; lost leg at Gettysburg; "American Scoundrel" (Grave 1906)

Section 7

Holmes, Oliver Wendell—Capt. in the 20th Mass.; Supreme Court Justice; "In our youth, our hearts were touched with fire" (Grave 7004)

Section 14

2nd Connecticut Heavy Artillery—Monument marks relative position of the unit as part of the capital defenses

Section 15

Longstreet, James Jr. & Robert—Sons of the Confederate general (Grave 32)

Parks, James—former slave at Arlington; only person born on the property who's also buried there (Grave 2)

Section 16

Confederate Memorial

Ezekiel, Moses—VMI cadet who fought at New Market; internationally renowned sculptor (Buried at base of Monument)

Section 31

Lincoln, Robert Todd—Son of President Lincoln; Secretary of War (Grave 13)

One Vast Cemetery

CHAPTER FOURTEEN

MAY 1864

ABOVE: The Wilderness of Virginia became one vast boneyard after major battles there in 1863 and 1864. (nps)

OPPOSITE: A grave's-eye view from the site of the former Wilderness Cemetery #2 offers a glimpse of the "dark, close wood." (cm)

There is just no hot like *Southern hot*, especially to a New England Yankee. The weather was typical for Virginia in the summer of '64: hot and muggy most of the day, every day. At some point there would be rain—but what kind of rain has huge drops that evaporate almost as soon as they reach the ground, that feel warm even as they hit your face? Virginia summer rain, that's what kind. A small bunch of us junior officers wandered over the ground where, only a year before, General Hunt had put his guns. Thank goodness he did, because they were all that had saved this ol' Army of the Potomac from certain death. That Stonewall Jackson of theirs . . . his infantry pretty much had their way about things during Chancellorsville. Now here we were again, more or less. Another year, another campaign, another general.

There was still plenty of what the historians call "debris of battle." Bits of faded uniforms—blue, gray, and butternut now all faded to a consistent grey-brown— more the color of dirt than of politics. Skulls, polished by the elements, lay carelessly on the ground, scattered along with longer leg bones, shorter arm bones, and an occasional bunch of ribs. Makes the human body seem real frail to see it just all bones like this. Some skeletons were covered with a little dirt, but it was pretty obvious that any sort of burial had been hasty and inefficient.

One of our group had been here the year before, when Hooker was in charge. He had some pretty strong opinions about this so-called Wilderness. He shared one now. "This region," he began, waving his arm to indicate the woods beyond us, "is an awful place to fight in. The utmost extent of vision is about one hundred yards. Artillery cannot be used effectively. The wounded are liable to be burned to death. I am willing to take my chances of getting killed, but I dread to have a leg broken and then to be burned slowly; and these woods will surely be burned if we fight here. I hope we will get through this chaparral without fighting,"

We sat in silence after this utterance. What else was there to say? We smoked our pipes, perched on the few structurally sound funeral mounds we could find and contemplated our bleak immediate futures. Unbeknownst to us, however, one of the private soldiers had been prying into the shallow graves with his bayonet. Suddenly, as if from the mysterious beyond, a grinning skull rolled to where we sat. A deep and spooky voice intoned, "This is what you are all coming to, and some of you will start toward it tomorrow!"

Damned infantry privates.

In the Wilderness, the fighting was so heavy "Anybody could get hit there," soldiers later lamented. (nps)

*   *   *

There was more than one battle in the area of eastern Virginia's second-growth forest known as the Wilderness. The first was the battle of Chancellorsville, May 1 to May 6, 1863. This was the principal engagement of the Chancellorsville campaign. Major General Joseph Hooker's Army of the Potomac fought against Robert E. Lee's Army of Northern Virginia. The fighting took place in an area of Virginia where tangled underbrush and trees had grown up in long-abandoned farmland. Close-quarters fighting among the dense woods created high casualties, but the battle proved a decisive Confederate victory, despite the difference in the size of their forces. Lee had commanded an army less than half the size of Hooker's.

The *Wilderness* itself deserves some explanation: it is a 70-square-mile piece of hell, or it was in the 1860s; a second-growth woodland; a "dark, close wood," according to South Carolina infantryman J. F. J. Caldwell. The area was in the process of regrowth after the initial colonial cutbacks of the 1700s. It had not yet developed a canopy layer to filter sunlight and restrict growth on the woodland floor, which was covered at that time in an undergrowth of low-growing shrubs, immature trees, and vines.

It was almost impossible to walk through the area,

and the floor itself would have been covered with forest debris—not a good place to march, fight, get wounded, or die. Sometimes the occasional marsh was hidden under the leaf cover; nasty quicksand that did not care a bit if its victim were alive or already dead. A Maine soldier wrote, "Blue and Gray sink side-by-side in its gloomy thickets and slimy pools."

Unfortunately, many soldiers had to maneuver in this geography. By the end of the battle of Chancellorsville, 30,764 men were casualties. Just how many were lost in the undergrowth is impossible to determine, because once a man went into that terrifying tangle, there was at least a 20 percent chance he would not come out again. A soldier inquired after a friend in another regiment:

With the woods aflame in more than a dozen places, soldiers from both sides scurried to save wounded soldiers from being burned to death. (loc)

They told us he had been shot thru' the arm, and had been sent to the rear, tho' his wound was severe, they thought it not serious, but that was the last that was ever known of Julius Root, whether he died from the loss of blood, or was caught in the forest fires that were raging about that time, and burned to death, or was taken prisoner by the enemy, and perished in some southern prison, will perhaps never be known. As the Sea does not give up its dead, so war does not yield its victims, and he sleeps, perhaps, in some quiet nameless grave . . . known only to Him who notes even the sparrow's fall, and who will summon him forth in that last great day.

The woods caught fire from the intensity of the constant shooting. First, a small curl of smoke drifted upward from the forest debris, centered, perhaps, around a spent minié ball. Then, a nourishing bit of fresh air caught the embers, fanning a flame from the kernel of fire and suddenly a conflagration began. A wounded man caught within these confines had little chance of getting out. As the battle continued, the Wilderness was transformed into a roaring inferno. The wounded and lost were trapped within its depths. Soldiers claimed afterward that they could see figures waving within the furnace, and a few braved the heat to pull out as many as possible. One Federal soldier described a rescue he attempted, "The fire was all around him. His eyes were big and blue, and his hair like raw silk surrounded by a wreath of fire. I heard him scream, 'Oh Mother. Oh God.' It left me trembling all over like a leaf." Many hundreds of soldiers burned to death.

Soldiers in the II Corps, marching to battle in May 1864, camped among the scattered remains of comrades who'd fought over the same ground in May of 1863 at the battle of Chancellorsville. (loc)

On any another battlefield, the casualties were easy to find. The killing ground was often described as a living thing—a squirming mass of wool-clad limbs, voices crying out for water or just for help. Stretcher-bearers found so many casualties that it was difficult to know where to begin trying to rescue the wounded, or later, remove the dead. In the Wilderness however, nothing was visible through the smoke of the black powder and the small fires that burned toward each other to join in an imitation of hell. The smoke caught beneath the leaves of the shrubs, and the flames immediately consumed any oxygen that might find itself coalescing.

No one knew exactly to whom the burned bodies belonged, and they stayed where they lay from May of 1863 to May 1864—a year of rain, wind, snow, and sun—to rot and bleach and become unidentifiable as Yank or Reb except by perhaps a burned button lying nearby, or by the place where the majority of their remains were found.

During the spring, a second battle was fought in this terrible place—the battle that has finally become known as the battle of the Wilderness. May 5 saw the start of Lt. Gen. Ulysses S. Grant's 1864 Overland Campaign against Lee. Again, fighting in such close quarters among the dense woods created high casualties, but the battle proved inconclusive for both sides. It produced an important strategic event, however: whereas before Union commanders had withdrawn their armies after failing to achieve victory south of the Rappahannock River, Grant did not retreat. Instead, he attempted to outflank Lee by moving to the left, setting the stage for the battle of Spotsylvania Courthouse just 12 scant miles down the road.

Grant's Overland Campaign began in almost exactly the same place where soldiers had fought a year earlier. The two-day battle of the Wilderness was bloody, confused, and uncoordinated. The growth was so thick, the smoke so dense, the fires beginning all over again— but this time, the soldiers of both armies tried to maneuver through the Wilderness with the sound of last year's bones crunching beneath their feet. One of Grant's officers referred to the whole sickening experience as "fighting in the shadow of death."

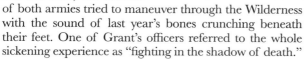

In the years after the war, travelers through the Wilderness found grim reminders of battle. (nps)

A soldier from the 11th North Carolina wrote that he took cover "behind a line of dead Federals so thick as to form a partial breastwork." One Union soldier saw a group of Confederates build a line of fortifications out of dead bodies: They "would lay a pile of dead men along then dig a trench and throw the dirt over the bodies serving the double purpose of burying their dead and building breastworks."

A hidden makeshift cemetery remained from Chancellorsville, where soldiers reported seeing even more human skulls, probably picked up in the woods and tossed over the palings to lie blanching among the graves. J. T. Trowbridge wrote in 1867, "Close by the southeast corner of the fence were three or four Rebel graves with old headboards . . . those buried there were North Carolinians . . . the graves were shallow, and the settling of the earth over the bodies had left the feet of one of the poor fellows sticking out."

Or were they real graves at all? "The arms in our possession, either captured from the enemy or belonging to our killed and wounded, were gathered up and broken or buried," said a Confederate artillerist; "and in order to deceive the enemy headboards were placed over them containing the names of fictitious soldiers."

Once again, the inconclusive results of the fight came at a very high cost for both armies, with an estimated combined total of 29,800 killed, wounded, and captured. And again, the horror of the battle was compounded by small brush fires that raged through the undergrowth, burning many wounded soldiers alive and filling the

After previous battles, the armies took time to tend to the wounded and collect the dead. The Overland Campaign had different rules—as it did in so many ways. Once Grant engaged Lee, he never let go, never giving Confederates the chance to catch their breath or reinforce. That also meant there was never enough time to gather up all the dead, who often lay where they fell even as the armies moved on in their death-grapple. (loc)

acreage with block powder smoke, wood smoke, and cries for help that could not be answered. Fresh rounds within the cartridge boxes still strapped to the belts of dead soldiers exploded in the flames. They blew "ghastly holes" in the midsections of their unfortunate wearers. A New York Zouave remembered the scene: "The almost cheerful *Pop! Pop!* of cartridges gave no hint of the . . . horror their noise bespoke. The bodies of the dead were blackened and burned beyond all recognition."

But Grant was not through just yet.

Union men knew the casualty figures had been devastating and expected another retreat, but instead Grant took his place at the head of the troops and turned the army toward Richmond. There would be no retreating this time.

Battle erupted again at Spotsylvania Courthouse, just beyond the borders of the dreaded Wilderness. The constant skirmishing and unrelenting contact between the armies was hard on men who were used to breaks between battles, but the armies endured.

An especially dark and dreadful test of endurance came on May 12. "The battle of Thursday was one of the bloodiest that ever dyed God's footstool with human gore," wrote one Confederate.

"I never expect to be fully believed when I tell of the horrors of Spotsylvania," a Union soldier echoed.

Night and day blended into one long horror story. "Rank after rank was riddled by shot and shell and bayonet-thrusts, and finally sank, a mass of torn and mutilated corpses," a member of Grant's staff wrote. "Then fresh troops rushed madly forward to replace the dead, and so the murderous work went on."

Even after that fight at the Mule Shoe, the armies stayed locked in combat. Bodies poorly buried—many times by simply being interred because they lay in front of some earthworks dug earlier—were unearthed by battle, sun, and rain. "Black bloated bodies were sitting up and reaching out from the earth," one soldier remembered. Another wrote, "The appearance of the dead who had been exposed to the sun so long was horrible in the extreme as we march past and over them—a sight never to be forgotten."

And it wasn't just the sight. "The stench which arose from them was so sickening and terrible that many of the men and officers became deathly sick from it," a Federal complained after nearly a week.

By May 21, the battle ended, but the armies moved on, leaving more destruction behind than ever before. The Army of the Potomac had suffered twice as many casualties as the Army of Northern Virginia since May 5, almost 35,000 in all.

Many of those casualties were still on the field in September 1864. One resident of Fredericksburg remembered:

> *Hundreds of dead Union soldiers were lying about, not at all putrefied, but darkened by the summer heat, still so life-like, that anybody who knew them would not have found any difficulty to recognize them. They obviously never had been touched, proven by the fact, that none of their pockets were turned inside out. There was nothing disagreeable about them, but by approaching them closely, they emitted an odor similar to stearin candles. I was particularly struck with the position of one corpse who behind the breastwork had his loaded musket to his shoulder, obviously taking aim. That these people had not been touched, much less buried, was only natural, as there were hardly any males left in that part of the country, the few remaining having enough to do with their own household & farm affairs. It happened however, that a few weeks later I took the same rout after we had some of the heavy fall rains, when the corpses appeared to be more or less decomposed, the one man mentioned before having lost his head, but otherwise retaining the same position.*

It was all someone else's problem now. The area known as the Wilderness remained one vast cemetery—as did much of central Virginia. When the Overland Campaign was finished, there would be 86,339 combined casualties scattered between the Rapidan and the James River.

The Skeleton Hunt

CHAPTER FIFTEEN

JUNE 1865

Amazingly, little was done about the dead after the battle of Chancellorsville, or after the battles of the Wilderness and, a dozen miles to the south, Spotsylvania. Perhaps it was just too overwhelming. Perhaps it was the land and the undergrowth itself that made properly taking care of casualties seem so impossible.

Injured soldiers who could be transported out were taken to care facilities in Richmond, Fredericksburg, and Washington. Otherwise, in May of 1864, the armies moved on, taking all their able-bodied men with them. There was no time for cleanup.

The real horrors of the Wilderness—no matter which battle—were the fires and the inaccessibility of the terrain. The wounded were left to burn or starve. No one heard their cries for help. A dead soldier lucky enough to be found at all was buried in hastily dug trenches. "Many Northern men were lying about . . ." wrote southerner St. George Tucker Bryan. "We had enough to do burying our own immortal dead and at this day I can see the two long trenches where they lay covered. We did not undertake to bury the dead horses. The smell from this battle was the worst I ever endured."

And so, the skeleton hunt began.

Local residents tried to bury bodies with some sense of dignity, but no coordinated effort was made until June 1865, after the war had ended. Even then, the job was a difficult one. "Two years after the battle [of the Wilderness] the ground was revisited by some officers who found many skeletons unburied in the thick woods, although a burial force under the direction of the War Department had undertaken the duty of covering all the remains," recalled then-retired Col. Charles L. Pierson of the 39th Massachusetts in 1905.

To commemorate Memorial Day each year, Fredericksburg National Cemetery holds a luminary ceremony. (cm)

Finally, in response to complaints about the unburied bodies left on the battlefields of the Wilderness area, the Federal government took some action—although it took more than a year for a coordinated effort to begin.

The 1st U.S. Veteran Volunteers arrived at Chancellorsville on June 11, 1865, and marched past the charred remains of the Chancellorsville house, the singular structure on the site. Scattered remnants of blankets, knapsacks, and other accouterments were evident even two years after the battle. By late afternoon, the 1st reached the Wilderness battlefield. They camped for the night on the northern end of the field. Local residents, hoping to trade their garden produce for anything these "new" soldiers carried in their knapsacks, immediately accosted them. William Landon, who fought at Fredericksburg as a member of the 14th Indiana, wrote, "All the rations we could spare were freely given them," but the demand exceeded the supply, and many went away hungry.

Makeshift cemeteries dotted Spotsylvania County's farms, forests, and fields. (nps)

Some of the veterans spoke to an old man with gray hair, his hand holding a hoe and his head trembling, and asked about the days immediately following May 7, 1864. The old gentleman described the comingled bones of horse and rider, and the possessions of the soldiers "from the envelope with its faint address in a woman's hand to the broken gun" scattered over the ground. He remembered the heaps of decaying knapsacks, piled together by companies of boys who would never return to collect them. "'Tis a gloomy sepulcher, where the trees, in tenderly covering with leaves the remains of the patriots, alone perform the last sad offices," the man lamented. "The wind moans through the pines, tears fall at home for them, but they sleep on, unconscious of a weeping nation. Ah, sir, there are thousands of both sides lying unburied in the Wilderness."

The Veteran Volunteers began collecting skeletons from the battle of the Wilderness on June 12. Starting at the northern end of the battlefield, they slowly worked their way south through "woods, thickets, fields, and swamps," searching for human remains. After going a certain distance, the soldiers would halt, change direction, then move forward again, marking the graves of those who had been properly interred and gathering up the remains of those who had not.

One out of every four men carried a sack to hold the bones. Skeletons that lay in marshy ground had not fully decomposed. Too offensive to handle, these were

buried where they lay. Although required to bury only
the Union dead, the Veteran Volunteers took it upon
themselves to inter Confederates as well. This nearly
doubled their workload.

Soldiers whose graves could be identified received
a simple headboard. Such was the case of John W.
Patterson, colonel of the 102nd Pennsylvania Volunteers,

who had died on May 5, 1864. Patterson's men had
committed his body to the ground and marked his grave
with whatever wood happened to be available at the time.
When Patterson's grave was found, more than a year later,
the rough headboard was replaced with a newer wooden
sign. Patterson's family later recovered his body and took
the marker home with them as a relic of his death.

Patterson was more fortunate than most. "It was
impossible to identify any of the bodies found unburied,"
insisted one of the 1st. "They having been exposed
[for] more than a year and all traces of identification
having been destroyed. . . ." Burial parties discovered
hundreds of soldier remains in the Wilderness. Those
who had been more properly buried were marked
with a new headboard. In three days of hunting, the
regiment collected thousands of bones and "a huge pile
of grinning, ghastly skulls." To hold the remains, the
soldiers constructed a cemetery south of the Orange
Turnpike, near the western edge of Saunders field. This
little graveyard was 60 feet square and enclosed by a
whitewashed fence made of horizontal planking. On one
of the fence posts workers nailed a board identifying it
as "Wilderness National Cemetery No. 1." "Wilderness
Cemetery No. 2" was created south of the Orange Plank
Road when the soldiers ran out of room in the first one.

The dead were buried in mass graves. Often as

**Wilderness Cemetery #1 sat
in a corner of Saunders Field
along the Orange Turnpike
(left). Wilderness Cemetery #2
sat near the spot where James
Longstreet had been wounded
along the Orange Plank Road
(right).** (nps)(nps)

Along the Fredericksburg Road in Spotsylvania, burial parties collected bodies for transport to Fredericksburg. (na)

many as 10 skulls were placed in each coffin, and the rest of the volume was filled with bones and bone fragments. Once filled, a top was screwed on to the wooden box and it was lowered into the ground by a "Corporal's Guard," offering as much dignity and ceremony as possible. "Unknown, but not unhonored nor unsung," wrote William Landon. Accounts differ, but between 180-350 men were interred in this first iteration of the Wilderness Military Cemetery. They were laid in neat and orderly rows, and over each box was erected a white wooden sign indicating that either unknown Union or Confederate remains lay below. When the National Cemetery at Fredericksburg was created in 1866, men buried at both Wilderness Cemeteries Number 1 and Number 2 were moved to that location. Only the depressions of the small burial plots in a corner of Saunders field remain today.

The 1st Veteran Volunteers were not the only participants in the skeleton hunt saga. Near Spotsylvania soldier graves were found near the Katherine Couse house, known as "Laurel Hill," which served as a makeshift Union hospital. "Many a poor fellow's bones rest here under the shade of the oak tree and pine, and few with boards to mark the spot," a survivor described in a letter to a friend. Captain John C. Brown, a veteran of the War of 1812, was the owner of "Liberty Hill," another home in the area. He and his family buried soldiers on that property as well. Colonel John Coons, of the 14th Indiana, was one of the few soldiers whose remains were identified and his burial site at Liberty Hill is marked with his name. Joseph Sanford was another local resident who helped inter the Union dead. He owned the

Spotsylvania Court House Hotel. When Gen. William T. Sherman and his armies passed through the area on their way to the Grand Review, Sanford obtained permission to bury the remains of as many soldiers as he could find at Spotsylvania. Sanford tackled his job with patriotic enthusiasm and had buried many of the corpses before the 1st Veteran Volunteers arrived. The few remaining were so decomposed and putrid that they were interred where they lay.

Even after the best efforts of the Veteran Volunteers and many others, the expedition was not truly considered a success. "Our 'Skeleton Hunt' has ended," William Landon wrote. "The heroes of the fierce and bloody battles of the Wilderness and Spotsylvania, who offered up their lives in defense of their country's honor and her flag in those terrible conflicts, are now, at last, reposing in peace beneath the 'sacred soil' of the Old Dominion."

Others disagreed. "Hundreds of graves on these battle fields are without any marks whatever to distinguish them, and so covered with foliage, that the visitor will be unable to find the last resting places of those who have fallen, until the rains and snows of winter wash from the surface the light covering of earth, and expose their remains." So wrote Capt. James M. Moore, assistant quartermaster, near the close of 1865.

Moore, who had been given the task of "superintending the interments of the remains of Union soldiers yet unburied and marking their burial places for future identification," found hundreds of skeletons as well as unmarked graves at the battlegrounds of the Wilderness and Spotsylvania. "By exposure to the weather, all traces of their identity were entirely obliterated," he wrote in his official report.

Three battles—four if one counts Fredericksburg— and many smaller skirmishes contributed to a mind-boggling number of dead in the aftermath of the battle. It's no wonder the National Park Service refers to it as "the bloodiest ground in America." Soldiers fought and refought over the same ground, the same battlefields, the same *de facto* cemeteries for years. Federal soldiers who attacked Marye's Heights at Second Fredericksburg on May 3, 1863, during the Chancellorsville campaign described poorly buried bodies from the preceding December's battle of Fredericksburg that had become partially disinterred. Marching into the Wilderness in

According to the National Park Service, a photographer took this photo on the west edge of Fredericksburg in 1864. In the right of the photo, the roof of a collapsed ice house tilts on the ground. "[The photographer] likely did not know that dozens of Union dead lay inside the ice house, thrown there by burial parties unwilling or unable to dig them proper graves," the Park Service says. "The bodies were removed to the National Cemetery after the war." (nps)

The hillside chosen for Fredericksburg National Cemetery had to be terraced in order to make enough space to accommodate all the graves. (nps)

early May of 1864, members of the Union II Corps camped among the bones of their fallen comrades from Chancellorsville a year earlier. At Spotsylvania on May 18, 1864, Federal troops recrossed the ground they had occupied on May 12, and the stench from the rain- and-sun-bloated bodies was so overpowering that some soldiers became ill during the attack on the Confederates.

That these battles were fought at or near the same geographic location makes the question "What did they do with all the bodies?" difficult to answer. With the carnage of the Wilderness and its adjoining areas, there is simply no way to tell if all the bodies have been found. It is hoped that all have been located and buried, even if not identified, but relic hunters, farmers, and homebuilders continue to disturb the land not protected by the state of Virginia or the National Park Service. Perhaps there are more to be found as the skeleton hunt continues.

At Fredericksburg National Cemetery

The front gate to the cemetery opens near the old caretaker's cottage just off the Sunken Road. The road, which runs along the base of Marye's Heights, was restored in 2004, so it once more resembles its wartime appearance. In 1901, Gen. Dan Butterfield had a monument to his V Corps troops placed in the cemetery, although his attacking force never reached that spot during the battle. (nps)

Today the terraced ground of the Fredericksburg National Cemetery holds the remains of 15,000 Union soldiers from the Civil War battles of Fredericksburg, Chancellorsville, the Wilderness, and Spotsylvania Courthouse. The first burials were performed by the citizens of Fredericksburg, who valiantly tried to put their war-shattered lives back together not once, but several times.

In July 1865, the land around Marye's Heights was designated a National Cemetery by the U. S. Congress.

The cemetery is part of the Fredericksburg and Spotsylvania National Military Park, the second-largest military park in the world, which encompasses the battlefields of Fredericksburg, Chancellorsville, Wilderness, and Spotsylvania, plus several historic buildings.

Chatham Manor, for instance, served as both a Union headquarters and a field hospital during the war. The names of famous people who served the wounded at Chatham include Walt Whitman, Clara Barton, Dorothea Dix and Dr. Mary Edwards Walker. The small house where Confederate General "Stonewall" Jackson died is also found on the grounds of the park complex.

A Union soldier's remains found at Kenmore Plantation in downtown Fredericksburg in November 1929 were reburied in the national cemetery on December 13, the 67th anniversary of the battle. (nps)

The cemetery grounds, adjacent to the Fredericksburg Battlefield Visitor Center, contain a number of interesting monuments dedicated to Union soldiers and their officers. The Fifth Corps Monument was dedicated in 1901. A monument to Colonel Joseph Moesch commemorates the gallant officer who died at the head of his regiment, the 83rd New York Volunteers, at the battle of the Wilderness. The center of the cemetery is marked by the Humphrey's Division Monument, dedicated to the Pennsylvania infantrymen of General Andrew Humphrey's division of the Fifth Corps. Over 1,000 of them led an unsuccessful attack on Marye's Heights against successfully entrenched Confederate troops.

Fredericksburg Cemetery was closed to interments in 1945, after adding the remains of 300 veterans from the Spanish-American War and both World Wars. The cemetery itself is open daily from dawn to dusk. For more information or to plan a trip, please check the Fredericksburg National Cemetery website: www.nps.gov/nr/travel/national_cemeteries/virginia/Fredericksburg_National_Cemetery.html

Guard towers looked down from beyond Andersonville's high stockade walls. Sightseers occasionally climbed to the platforms to gawk at the prisoners. (cm)

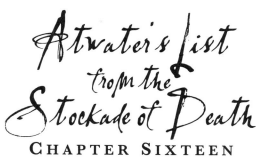

Atwater's List from the Stockade of Death

CHAPTER SIXTEEN

JUNE 1865

Dorence Atwater (above) kept secret information about the dead of Andersonville Prison, but in the weeks of the war's close, the Federal government didn't want to listen to what he had to say. (nps)

"Oh my dear, whatever is this going to be about?" wondered the forty-four year old woman as she heard the ascent of thumping footsteps rushing up the three floors of stairs to her small office in Washington City. Clara Barton pushed her chair from her tiny, paper-strewn desk and threaded her way through the maze of boxes and bags of supplies meant for Union hospitals, maneuvering her narrow hoops as she went. She got to the paneled, wooden door just as the young man on the other side began his insistent knocking.

"Yes? Yes? May I help you?" she said as she opened the door. Tiny Miss Barton looked up—and then up some more—into the fiery eyes of a very tall, very young-appearing former Union soldier.

Dorence Atwater was still very thin, but determination overrode any suggestion that he was also frail. He had been released from Camp Sumter, more commonly known as Andersonville Prison, just that February, in 1865. Frail, indeed.

Atwater had enlisted early in the war, serving in the 2nd New York Cavalry, until the battle of Gettysburg, where he was captured. An entire year passed in one Confederate hellhole after another. His confinement in Richmond's Belle Isle had been hounded by recurrent bouts of severe diarrhea. Though ill, young Atwater quickly realized that getting up and moving about was much healthier than lying in a hospital bed, so he volunteered as a prison hospital clerk in exchange for parole.

Two portions of Andersonville's outer stockade have been rebuilt, including the imposing entrance gate. (cm)

When he was transferred to Andersonville, the diarrhea accompanied him. By May 1865, Atwater was again sent to the prison hospital, which at the time of his admission was located inside the bounds of the stockade. Remembering the lessons he learned at Belle Isle, Private Atwater approached Confederate surgeon Dr. Isaiah White about accepting parole to work as a hospital clerk. On June 15, his offer was accepted, and Dorence Atwater became one of several prisoners tasked with maintaining the Andersonville death register.

By late August, Atwater began his project: he made double copies of the death list. He had been in Confederate prisons long enough to know that the South kept terrible records, and he believed that the Confederate command would never turn over an accurate copy of the main list under any circumstances.

Atwater's suspicions were well founded. He smuggled his personal list out when he left the prison, in late February 1865. By mid March, he was paroled home to Connecticut, still in possession of the list. Within a month, the war had ended. Atwater notified the federal government about his idea to go back to Georgia and try to identify and mark the prison graves, but interest was lukewarm.

Impatient with the vague promise of some sort of "expedition" from the government, Dorence Atwater pondered his dilemma. Then he went to Washington.

By the time Atwater finished his tea in Room 9— Miss Barton's small, jumbled parlor on 7th Street and her makeshift Missing Soldiers Office—Clara was convinced.

Barton's cleft chin was only a physical symbol of her determination to help *her* soldiers and their families. "I have an almost complete disregard of precedent, and a faith in the possibility of something better," she said. "It irritates me to be told how things have always been done. I defy the tyranny of precedent."

In late July and early August 1865, Miss Clara Barton and Mr. Dorence Atwater accompanied the army's expedition to mark and establish Andersonville National Cemetery.

When the expedition retuned to Washington, Atwater took his list back from the military, eager to publish it so that family members might know of the fate of their loved ones. The Andersonville Death Register was published in the *New York Tribune* in 1866. It created a stir of notoriety, and almost immediately Atwater was charged with larceny. He was court martialed and sent to prison.

Outraged, Clara Barton brought all her power to bear upon President Andrew Johnson, and her friend was released after serving three months. Atwater went to work with Barton, and the two spent much of their time going through burial records and writing letters to families of the dead. He and Barton toured the Northeast lecturing on Andersonville and raising money for the Missing Soldiers Office. As Atwater had suspected, for many families, this was the first notification that their loved ones had died at Andersonville.

Atwater's list was used to identify the dead at Andersonville and to label the markers in the cemetery, making Pvt. Dorence Atwater one of the most important enlisted soldiers in the aftermath of battle. Thanks to his work and the work of other paroled clerks to maintain accurate records of deaths in prison camps—and to their courage to secretly copy those lists and sneak them out—nearly ninety-five percent of the prisoner graves at Andersonville were identified.

Dorence Atwater became a consul for the Sate Department in the 1870s. He was first stationed in the Seychelles Islands, but eventually he was transferred to Tahiti. After his retirement, he became a well-respected businessman and married a member of Tahiti's royal family. He died in 1910 in San Francisco, but was given a royal funeral in his adopted home, Tahiti.

Among Andersonville's many monuments, one recognizes the work of Clara Barton, who did much through the American Red Cross to ensure the remains of Andersonville's victims were properly identified. The monument was erected in 1915 by the Women's Relief Corps, an auxiliary of the Grand Army of the Republic. (cm)

*   *   *

Early in the war it did not take long for a prisoner to get exchanged, or traded, for a prisoner from the other side. Once in a while, someone who had been captured at a time or in a place inconvenient for transporting a prisoner could be paroled. This meant being provisionally released upon giving his word that he would not take up arms against the enemy until having been notified of a formal exchange with an enemy captive of equal rank.

By late 1862, both sides realized that exchanging and paroling prisoners was prolonging the war by returning men to the ranks. When the Confederacy

Wooden headboards originally marked the graves of bodies in Andersonville National Cemetery. (nps)

threatened to treat African-American prisoners more harshly than white prisoners, Abraham Lincoln halted all prisoner exchanges. It was at this time that prisons began to be constructed for the specific purpose of holding enemy detainees.

The most notorious prison of them all, Andersonville in southwest Georgia, opened in February 1864. By June 1865, it was still nothing more than a twenty-six acre rectangle surrounded by a fifteen-foot high stockade fence, bisected by the remnants of a small stream. In the words of Ransom Chadwick, a member of the 85th New York Infantry who arrived with other men of his regiment on April 30, 1864, the spectacle upon entering the prison, "almost froze our blood with horror, and made our hearts fail within us. Before us were forms that had once been active and erect, *stalwart men*, now nothing but mere walking skeletons, covered with filth and vermin."

During the fourteen months of its existence, 45,000 prisoners were brought to Andersonville. Nearly 13,000 died within its walls, and many who were able to leave died soon thereafter. Those who survived often led shortened lives due to the permanent injury to their systems left by starvation, dysentery, scurvy, hookworm, exposure, and psychological maltreatment. A federal military tribunal tried Henry Wirz, the commandant of the inner stockade at Andersonville, on charges of conspiracy and murder. He was found guilty. On November 10, 1865 he was hanged for his war crimes. Wirz was one of only two Confederates sentenced to die for their part in the Civil War.

In 1865, the mass graves of prisoners next to Andersonville Prison became a national cemetery. A month later, Barton and Atwater's team started their work surveying the cemetery. The prison itself, though,

Andersonville National Cemetery remains in use as a burial place for more recent veterans and their wives. Two Medal of Honor recipients are buried there: James Wiley, who captured a Confederate flag at the battle of Gettysburg on July 3, 1863, and Luther H. Story, for action in the Korean War on September 1, 1950. (cm)

returned to private ownership and fell into disrepair.

In 1890, the Georgia chapters of the Grand Army of the Republic purchased the site of Andersonville Prison through membership and subscriptions. The Women's Relief Corps, an auxiliary to the GAR, donated the site to the federal government in 1910.

In 1970, Congress designated the Andersonville a National Historic Site and transferred its management to the National Park Service. In 1988, the national Prisoner of War Museum opened at Andersonville as a monument to all Americans who have served as prisoners of war. The museum serves as the Visitors Center to the entire Andersonville complex. There is ongoing archeological work being done on the grounds, and exhibits of art, video, photographs and other displays are constantly upgraded and changed. Two sections of the stockade walls have been reconstructed, as has the North Gate and the northeast corner.

The Andersonville National Cemetery is divided into seventeen sections, with most of the burials from its prison history in sections E, F, H, J, and K. Between 1905 and 1916, nine states erected monuments honoring those who died while being held at Andersonville: Maine, Pennsylvania, Connecticut, Illinois, Indiana, Iowa, New Jersey, New York, and Minnesota. More recently constructed monuments include the Georgia Monument, dedicated in 1976 to commemorate all American POWs and a memorial to the men held in German POW Camp Stalag 17 during World War II.

To plan a trip to Andersonville National Historic Site, please contact the park at 229-924-0343 or visit the website at www.nps.gov/nr/travel/national_cemeteries/Georgia/Andersonville_National_Cemetery.html.

Hollywood: A Reinterment Story

CHAPTER SEVENTEEN

JUNE 13, 1953

"Missus Freeman, Missus Freeman—come quick," the maid called. "It's the doctor. He's in his study, and he's just not answering me. I asked him if he wanted a cup of coffee and some fruit for his lunch, but he isn't answering. . . ."

The morning of June 13, 1953, began differently than other mornings at Westbourne, the Georgian Revival-style mansion purchased by the Freeman family in 1938. Dr. Douglas Southall Freeman usually awoke around 3:30 in the morning and followed a strictly scripted schedule until an early bedtime of about 9 p.m. "A wise use of time," he said, made the difference "between drudgery and happiness, between existence and career."

But today was different. The long trek up two long flights of stairs to Freeman's third-story writing study confirmed what his wife suspected after the maid came to her: Douglas Southall Freeman was dead of a heart attack at age 67.

The native Virginian, the son of a Confederate veteran, the man who had won the 1935 Pulitzer Prize for his four-volume biography of Confederate Robert E. Lee, would be buried a few days later in Hollywood Cemetery among the finest of Virginia's native sons and daughters.

* * *

The story of Richmond, Virginia's Hollywood Cemetery does not begin with the Civil War. It opened in 1849, and was initially planned to occupy land known

Historian Douglas Southall Freeman (above) did more than nearly anyone to enshrine the memory of the South. He is buried in Richmond's Hollywood Cemetery among the Confederate heroes he so revered. (nps)(cm)

as "Harvie's Woods." Its name—Hollywood—came from the abundance of tree holly in the area. Prior to the 1840s, formal burial was restricted to family plots and churchyards. Graves in these dreary places had little room for sunlight or vegetation. Nothing encouraged either a family member or a passerby to stop and remember, or appreciate. A churchyard was a sad, lonely place.

American presidents James Monroe (left) and John Tyler (right) are buried in Hollywood Cemetery's Presidents' Circle. (cm)(cm)

As populations increased, burial grounds began to be located outside the town and no longer on church grounds. In 1831, Boston's beautiful garden-style Mount Auburn became the first American cemetery of the Romantic rural cemetery movement. A rural cemetery was designed with a vision: to provide a place of sanctuary, solitude, quiet contemplation, adornment, and beauty for the dead, and for those who came to contemplate past and future. After 1849, Richmond, Virginia, had her own contemplative garden cemetery. Locals were the first interred in the new burial grounds, but on July 4 1858—the anniversary of his death—the remains of President James Monroe were reinterred at Hollywood. He was buried in the "President's Circle," the first of many important people to be buried in this lovely necropolis.

By 1863, the cemetery was already one of the largest for Southern Civil War burials due to its proximity to Richmond, the Confederate capital, and the battlegrounds of Virginia. Soldier interments continued at Hollywood through April 1865.

By June, the official killing work was done, but the South was a vast charnel house of unburied or poorly buried bodies. Many more just decomposed where they fell, unknown, unaccounted for, Union and Confederate. The Federal government got to work finding Union soldier remains, and hundreds of thousands of dollars were appropriated for disinterment and reburial in places soon organized as National Cemeteries. The work *had* to proceed quickly. The longer bodies were left without a proper burial, the more difficult they became to identify.

It soon became painfully clear that hundreds of thousands of soldiers lay in undocumented locations. Their remains were untended, unmarked, and their deaths unrecorded. No family knew where a missing loved one might lie, and the government did not know either. The loyal states of the North had a stable government and a plan for dealing with the problem, but the states so lately in rebellion were too overwhelmed to consider any solution. The Federal government, under the influence of Radical Reconstruction, felt it was only responsible for Yankee soldiers. It was not until early in 1866 that a comprehensive reburial program was seen as necessary for the South as well as the North. By then, white Southerners were outraged at the attitude of the federal government concerning the burial of Confederate soldiers. The *Richmond Examiner* declared that Northerners were wrong! Was a man who had worn the grey "less a hero because he failed? No! He is *ours*—and shame be to us if we do not care for his ashes."

Confederate President Jefferson Davis, originally buried in New Orleans' Metairie Cemetery in Mississippi, was moved by his wife to Hollywood Cemetery in 1893 so that he would remain in the capital of the Confederacy he once administered. (cm)

That spring, a group of upper-class Richmond women responded to the *Examiner's* call. The Hollywood Memorial Association of the Ladies of Richmond was founded, and it was ready to meet the challenge. Mrs. William McFarland, president of the Association, understood that one of the problems—"the city is begirt with an army of Confederate dead"—was also one of its solutions. Richmond had two nearby cemeteries, and plenty of empty land adjoining them. Lovely, rural Hollywood Cemetery lay to the west of the city, and the more traditional Oakwood lay to the east. Oakwood was conveniently close to the grounds where Chimborazo, the largest military hospital in the South, had stood.

The immediate problem was to clean up and restore the 11,000-plus soldiers' graves dug at Hollywood during the war. The next step was to gather the hundreds of Confederate dead surrounding the area and reinter them into hallowed and protected ground. Local farmers were hired to scour battle sites on the Richmond outskirts for bodies and bring them to Hollywood Cemetery during the summer and fall of 1866. Momentum increased as private donations and fund-raising activities publicized the cause. Contributions also came from the legislatures of other former Confederate states whose men lay on Virginia soil.

Whereas in the North, the job of reburial was far removed from the lives of most citizens, in the South the job fell to citizen efforts almost entirely. White Southern women mobilized their constituent groups far beyond the immediate purposes of burial and bereavement. Many claim that southern women created the first Decoration Days, where the graves of the Confederate soldiers were trimmed and decorated with spring flowers, although several groups vie for this honor. The reburial and adoption of the graves of the grey was much more than a private, familial obligation—it was an act both public and political. Had Southern men begun the efforts, it would have been seen for what historian Drew Gilpin Faust calls "a means of perpetuating southern resistance to northern domination and to the reconstruction of southern society." Southern women, on the other hand, were an integral part of the creation of Confederate memory. It was into their gentle, white hands that the memory of the Lost Cause was entrusted.

Matthew Fontaine Maury, the father of modern oceanography, is buried atop one of Hollywood's many rolling hills. (cm)

> *Sleep sweetly in your humble graves,*
> *Sleep, martyrs of a fallen cause!—*
> *Though yet no marble column craves*
> *The pilgrim here to pause.*
>
> *Stoop, angels, hither from the skies!*
> *There is no holier spot of ground,*
> *Than where defeated valor lies,*
> *By mourning beauty crowned*

— from "Ode" by Henry Timrod

*   *   *

One immediate difference between rural or garden-style Hollywood Cemetery and other cemeteries is that there are very few rows of identical headstones lined up one after the other. Instead, Hollywood flows in a labyrinthine style, like a meander through the Virginia woodlands. It can be visited by walking, taking a self-guided car tour, a trolley ride or on a Segway. The cemetery contains many points of interest, including several large dogs, a Frog Shrine, and the alleged crypt of the Richmond Vampire, but of interest to Civil War students are the Pyramid, the Confederate Section, and the numerous graves of Confederate heroes and U.S. presidents with Southern roots.

Hollywood's winding paths overlook the James River in an inviting, 135-acre ramble. (cm)

The former President of the Confederate States of America, Jefferson Davis, is one of the most famous

Southerners reinterred at Hollywood Cemetery. United States Presidents James Monroe, John Tyler, and their wives are also buried there, as are 25 Confederate generals, including George Pickett and J. E. B. Stuart. Oceanographer Matthew Fontaine Maury, the "Patherfinder of the Seas," is buried there, as is Dr. Hunter Holmes McGuire, Stonewall Jackson's surgeon.

Several Virginia governors, politicians, and Supreme Court justices also rest in Hollywood.

However, as Douglas Southall Freeman pointed out a generation later, "The greatest events in Richmond were the funerals of military heroes, when torches burned at midnight and the Stonewall band came down from Staunton, and all the stalwarts of the great city put on gray jackets again."

No figure in the twentieth century did more to carry on the work of Southern remembrance than Freeman, who, after a private family ceremony, joined Jefferson Davis, J. E. B. Stuart, George Pickett, and other Confederate leaders—men whose legendary reputations he helped cement—in Richmond's Hollywood Cemetery. His grave sits alongside that of his wife, Inez Virginia Goddin Freeman, who was buried on the little knoll in 1974.

Despite all the other people buried in Hollywood, though, in many ways it is a Civil War cemetery—or at least parts are. The post-war reinterment movement

Fitzhugh Lee not only served as governor of Virginia after the war, he was one of three former Confederate officers to be called into active service with the United States Army during the war with Spain. He eventually retired in 1901 as a brigadier general in the U.S. Army. He died in 1905. (cm)

made it possible for many families to identify their kin, or at least to visit a cemetery and decorate someone's final resting place. Civil War soldier graves marked "Unknown" receive a flag or a luminary once in a while. There is a strange power in their very anonymity. These are not sad clusters of family tombstones in local churchyards. The movement to rebury the bodies of Civil War soldiers created families of men related to each other by the war. The bodies underneath the tombstones are brothers in arms.

At Hollywood Cemetery

There are many reasons to pay a visit to Richmond, Virginia's beautiful Hollywood Cemetery, but spending time in a nineteenth century rural, garden-style burial ground is reason enough. If the word *cemetery* calls forth images of rows of identical tombstones, or a lawn so flat it can easily be mowed without concern for a grave marker, then prepare to be amazed. Hollywood Cemetery is skillfully planned. It uses the natural beauty of rolling Virginia hillsides to create stunning views, among which nestle the monuments and markers of history.

For the first-time visitor, a guided tour is suggested; otherwise, use a map and a car to find specific areas of interest. Segway tours seem to be popular, too. Check the lovely, easy-to-navigate Hollywood Cemetery website for all pertinent information as well as a Schedule of Events at www.hollywoodcemetery.org.

A detailed map of the cemetery, available from the front offices, guides you to a variety of interesting, and often amusing, sites. Fifth United States President James Monroe is buried inside an elaborate wrought-iron open sarcophagus; the tomb is a U.S. National Historic Landmark. Originally, he was interred in New York at the Gouverneur family vault but came to the President's Circle 27 years later, in 1858.

Tenth President John Tyler, "His Accidency" (due to becoming president upon the death of William Henry Harrison), also resides in the President's Circle. A tall, dark obelisk marks his tomb. A smaller monument to Tyler is placed directly at the front of the much taller one. When the first Southern states seceded in 1861, Tyler led a compromise movement; failing, he worked actively to create the Southern Confederacy. He died on January 18, 1862, a member of the Confederate House of Representatives. "Under other circumstances, a feeling of regret might have pervaded the entire country," said the *New York Herald*, "but his treachery to the Union and its laws will prevent those persons in the North . . . from experiencing sorrow at his demise. He had been Chief Magistrate of the glorious Union, to the destruction of which he devoted the last ill-spent hours of his life." After his death, Confederate President Jefferson Davis escorted Tyler's remains to Hollywood Cemetery.

The Jefferson Davis Circle is the resting place of Confederate President Jefferson Davis and his family. Initially Davis was buried in New Orleans where he died, but on Memorial Day, 1893, he was reburied in Virginia, with the rest of his family. The Davis Circle now contains the remains of four-year-old Joseph Davis, who fell from the porch of the Confederate White House in 1864. Margaret Davis Hayes, Jefferson and Varina Davis's oldest daughter, Mary, is buried within the Circle, as is Varina Anne "Winnie" Davis, the "Daughter of the Confederacy," who carried the burden of living up to the image imposed upon her by an adoring southern public. She died at 34. Jefferson Davis, Jr., died of yellow fever when he was 21, and Jefferson Davis's second wife, Varina Howell Davis, joined the Circle at her death in 1906.

J. E. B. Stuart's grave marker is a tall white obelisk surrounded by the much smaller markers of his wife and three children. (cm)

Within Davis Circle are several iconic mortuary pieces: the angels that guard the resting places of Winnie and Mary; the broken column that marks the burial place of Jefferson Davis, Jr.; and the small stone that marks Joseph's burial. The children of Richmond donated it soon after young Joe fell to his death. A life-sized bronze statue represents Jefferson Davis himself.

The Monument to the Confederate War Dead is a 90-foot-tall square pyramid that stands in the Soldiers' Section of the cemetery, built to honor the 18,000-plus Confederate enlisted men buried nearby.

The Hollywood Memorial Association of the Ladies of Richmond raised more than $28,000 to erect this unusual monument, designed by engineer Charles Henry Dimmock. Made of chiseled James River granite, it is held together by artful stonework—no mortar was used. The stones were added using a crane. When it was time to place the capstone, the crane was not quite tall enough. Placing the stone was considered a very dangerous job. It was offered to Thomas Stanley, a Gamble's Hill convict working on the Pyramid with the construction crew. Evidently the knots in the hoisting ropes were tied too close to the top, preventing the stone from passing farther up the rope. Stanley poured warm water on the tie lines, shrinking them the necessary inches. Then, as a breathless crowd gathered and watched, the former horse thief put himself between the triangular hanging rock and the rest of the structure, and righted the stone. It settled perfectly into its seat atop the pyramid. Legend claims Stanley was granted his freedom for the success of his efforts, but there is no proof of this; it merely says "transferred" next to his name in later prison records.

The towering presence of the Monument to the Confederate War Dead can be seen from many areas within Hollywood, reminding visitors of the brave Confederate heroes buried there. (cm)

Latin inscriptions appear on two sides of the pyramid. They read, *Memoria in Aeterna* and *Numini et Patri Astro*. Read together, they translate to, "In eternal memory of those who stood for God and Country." The Pyramid was the first memorial erected to the "Lost Cause," and it dominates the Confederate Soldiers' Section.

The Soldiers' Section is divided into smaller areas named for the various places where Civil War remains were gathered. One of the most visited is "Gettysburg Hill." More than 2,000 bodies were reinterred in 1872—mainly the men from Pickett's Charge. Since so many of these men had been under his command on July 3, 1863, Confederate Gen. George Pickett chose to be buried on the hill with his men. His monument is a small temple set atop a rough brick base.

Twenty-five Civil War generals in all are buried at Hollywood, including J. E. B. Stuart, Fitzhugh Lee, Henry Heth, and John Pegram. One of the most compelling is Confederate Brig. Gen. Richard Brooke Garnett. Garnett was one of the few who were mounted during Pickett's Charge. He was ill and did not think he could walk the mile distance on foot. Garnett rode toward Cemetery Ridge, and never returned. His riderless horse was found wandering the battlefield later in the day, but Garnett's remains were never identified. A marble marker on Gettysburg Hill, in the Confederate Soldiers' Section of Hollywood Cemetery, reads:

> *Among the Confederate Soldiers's Graves in this area is the probable resting place of Brigadier General Richard Brooke Garnett, C. S. A. who was killed in action July 3, 1863, as he led his Brigade in the charge of Pickett's Division on the final day of the Battle of Gettysburg. First buried on the battlefield, General Garnett's remains were likely removed to this area in 1872 along with other Confederate dead brought from Gettysburg by the Hollywood Memorial Association.* Requiescat in Pace. *Richard Brooke Garnett 1817-1863.*

The address is 412 South Cherry Street, in Richmond, Virginia. Contact information is online at hollywoodcemetery.org.

The Last Civil War Veteran

CHAPTER EIGHTEEN

AUGUST 2, 1956

Last Union Army Veteran Dies Drummer at 17, He Lived to 109

Albert Woolson of Duluth Also Was Sole Survivor of Grand Army of Republic

February 1, 1847-August 2, 1956

Duluth, Minn., Aug. 2--Albert Woolson, the last member of the Civil War's Union Army, died today at the age of 109. . . .

* * *

The aftermath of battle became the aftermath of the Civil War. After more than 750,000 deaths between 1861 and 1865, Civil War veterans went back to their homes and families and tried to put their lives back together. North and South, many veterans enjoyed the company of their fellow veterans and created groups like the Sons of Confederate Veterans and the Grand Army of the Republic. These organizations held annual "encampments" or large meetings where all soldiers met, from officers to enlisted, to catch up on current events, to re-fight battles, and to remember the camaraderie that had held their respective armies together.

Each year there were fewer and fewer in attendance at these get-togethers. The average age of a Union soldier in the Civil War was twenty-six years old; while there is no definite information on Confederate soldiers, the end of the war saw old men and young boys pressed into

As the oldest surviving member of the Grand Army of the Republic, Albert Woolson (above) was immortalized in bronze atop the G.A.R. memorial at Gettysburg National Battlefield (opposite). (mg)(dd)

Southern service. If a soldier served three or four years, he would be nearing thirty when he finally took off his uniform. By the turn of the century, then, most veterans who had survived that long were sixty-five or older.

Unfortunately, death took some of these men earlier than perhaps otherwise, for the war had left scars upon constitutions that were not always physically evident. Digestive systems had been wracked by chronic dysentery. Prolonged marching and continued exposure to the elements had weakened muscular, immune, and endocrine systems. Alcohol and disease had done damage, as had incarceration for any extended length of time. Few soldiers ate a healthy diet, which affected growth and development from their twenties onward. Of course, there was no diagnosis for Post Traumatic Stress Syndrome, but many men had regularly occurring episodes of *soldier's heart*, which was the same thing.

The men tried to take care of each other, just as they had during the war. In many cases, when one died, he was laid to rest by his local band of brothers, and the government paid for a marble marker to show where he slumbered.

Only nationally known men receive national mourning. The national grieving process that first occurred with the death of Col. Elmer Ellsworth in May 1861 repeated itself after four years of almost unending grief with the death of President Abraham Lincoln. Lincoln's remains were borne from Washington City to Springfield, Illinois, on a special funeral train that was welcomed no matter what time of day or night it travelled through a town. Poet Walt Whitman wrote:

Albert Woolson enlisted as a 17-year-old drummer boy. Later in life, he revisited his drummer boy days to the delight of admirers. (mg)

> *Coffin that passes through lanes and streets,*
> *Through day and night with the great cloud darkening*
> *   the land,*
> *With the pomp of the inloop'd flags, with the cities*
> *   draped in black,*
> *With the show of the States themselves as if crape-veil'd*
> *   women standing,*
> *With processions long and winding and the flambeaus*
> *   of the night,*
> *With the countless torches lit, with the silent sea of faces*
> *   and the unbared heads,*
> *With the waiting depot, the arriving coffin,*
> *   and the sombre faces,*
> *With dirges through the night, with the thousand voices*

rising strong and solemn,
With all the mournful voices of the dirges pour'd around
the coffin,
The dim-lit churches and the shuddering organs--
where amid these you journey,
With the tolling tolling bells' perpetual clang,
Here, coffin that slowly passes,
I give you my sprig of lilac.

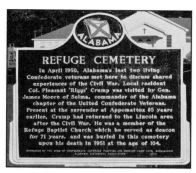

General Robert E. Lee's death, only five years after the war, was mourned all over the South, and those who had worn the blue paid tribute to a gallant foe. "Lee was not a man of one section of the country or of one time," eulogized Kentucky Senator and former Union brigadier general John W. Finnell," but rather a man who belonged to all of the country and all ages."

Fifteen years later, the death of General-then-President Ulysses S. Grant presented another chance for national mourning on a massive scale. 125,000 people lined up to look upon his face as he laid in state in New York City's City Hall. This event was only rivaled by the funeral procession on Broadway for Abraham Lincoln twenty years earlier.

General William T. Sherman died in 1891. In a joint meeting of Congress, Sen. Charles Fridlender, who had served under Sherman during the war, remarked:, "We who . . . fought under him loved him as only soldiers can love the man who leads them to victory, and the title Uncle Billy . . .was the expression of the love we bore him."

Sherman was carried to his grave, following a huge, well-attended funeral, by Confederate general Joseph E. Johnston, among others. The funeral took place on a cold, wet February day, and Johnston stood in sadness, his head uncovered for his friend Sherman. A fellow mourner urged the elderly Johnston to put on his hat. Johnston refused. "If I were in his place and he were standing in mine he would not put *his* hat on, Johnston said. A month later, Johnston himself was dead of pneumonia caught during Sherman's funeral, and once again, the South mourned.

*   *   *

With the passing of years, the G.A.R.s, as they came to be called, became older men and finally old men. Their fellow countrymen seemed to recall them only on Memorial Day. They wore the blue uniform coat and slouch hat of the G.A.R. and marched in the parades as long as they could.

Finally, they became very old men sitting quietly in the sun. There were other veterans of later wars who had their own stories to tell.

By 1938, very few Civil War veterans were left. Those

It is known for certain that Albert Woolson was the last remaining veteran, Union or Confederate. There are some problems with identifying the last remaining Confederate, though, and controversy still swirls around a few of those contending for the place of honor. A thorough checking of both birth and death records as well as military records concludes that the most likely candidate was Pleasant "Riggs" Crump. Crump served as a private in Company A, 10th Alabama, and was present at the surrender at Appomattox Court House. He was born December 23, 1847 and died December 31, 1951, making him just over 104 years old. (fag)

who remained seemed like fragile relics of a time gone by, worthy of honor simply by virtue of their survival.

That year, on July 3, Oak Hill in Gettysburg, Pennsylvania, was the location of a special service marking

the seventy-fifth anniversary of the battle there. Of the 250,000 who attended the installation of the Eternal Light Peace Memorial, 1,800 were veterans. Another president was there to say some words. Franklin Roosevelt compared the task of the boys of '61 to the men of his day: "All of them we honor, not asking under which Flag they fought then--thankful that they stand together under one Flag now." In less than five years, the sons and grandsons of Civil War veterans would be standing side-by-side, facing together international enemies in World War II.

Union and Confederate veterans had *all* gotten a lot grayer by the time of the big reunion in Gettysburg in 1938. (loc)

For those 1,800 veterans, it was to be the last big reunion. All of them were at least in their nineties. These frail old men were all that was left to remind America of her second great struggle. Each veteran that died made that chain of connection to the past even more tenuous.

By August 1956, former Pvt. Albert Woolson was the last man standing. He was 109. In October of 1864, Woolson had enlisted in Company C, First Minnesota Volunteer Heavy Artillery. He, his drum, and his bugle served with the Army of the Tennessee, commanded by Maj. General George Thomas.

Woolson had spent most of the summer of 1956 hospitalized—nine weeks—with a recurring lung congestion condition. He lapsed into a coma five days before his death and did not regain consciousness. Members of his family were at his bedside when he died in St. Luke's Hospital, Duluth, Minnesota, on August 2. At his death, Woolson was receiving a pension of $135 a month. He got no other benefits, but had been entitled to hospitalization and outpatient care.

On August 6, Woolson was laid to rest in the family plot in Park Hill Cemetery. More than 1,500 persons attended the afternoon funeral in the Duluth Armory, while hundreds more lined the route to the cemetery. Some 2,000 watched as the bronze casket was interred with full military honors. The New York *Times* published

Last Union Army Veteran Dies; Drummer at 17, He Lived to 109

Albert Woolson of Duluth Also Was Sole Survivor of Grand Army of Republic

By The Associated Press.

DULUTH, Minn., Aug. 2—Albert Woolson, the last member of the Civil War's Union Army, died today at the age of 109.

Mr. Woolson, who answered President Lincoln's call to arms and marched off to war as a drummer boy when he was 17, had been hospitalized for nine weeks with a recurring lung congestion condition. He lapsed into a coma early Saturday and did not regain consciousness. Since then, he had been fed intravenously and received oxygen through a nasal tube.

Members of his family were at his bedside when he died in St. Luke's Hospital.

Full-scale military funeral services will be conducted at the National Guard Armory here Monday at 2 P. M. Burial will be in the family lot at Park Hill Cemetery here.

Only three veterans of the

Continued on Page 19, Column 2

Albert Woolson Associated Press, 1933

Albert Woolson's obituary appeared on the front page of *The New York Times.* (nyt)

an obituary about Albert Woolson featuring a statement by then-President Dwight David "Ike" Eisenhower:

> *The American people have lost the last personal link with the Union Army. His passing brings sorrow to the hearts of all of us who cherished the memory of the brave men on both sides of the War Between the States.*

In our day, we are losing our World War II veterans, and at some point, the men and women now returning from duty in the Middle East will pass for their own Final Review. The cries of "Remember Ellsworth" seem like a clarion call for the remembrance of all our veterans. The question "What did they do with the bodies?" was never more relevant than it is at a time amputations are being performed on U. S. soldiers at rates rivaling those of the 1860s.

Interest in the American Civil War does not appear to be slowing down. More books are published annually about the war than about any other conflict. These publications help remind us that those who fought deserve to be remembered: Confederate or Union, officer or enlisted, identified or still unknown. That is what *we* now do with all the bodies—we read about them and remember their stories and their sacrifices. We remember they were ordinary people just like us, trying their best to do their duty under extraordinary circumstances.

May they all rest in peace.

Albert Woolson's monument was dedicated on September 12, 1956. "This statue is in many ways unique," said the commander of the G.A.R. during his speech at the dedication. "Usually statues are dedicated to great and noble men, great military leaders, or men who have given their lives for their country. Here we have a statue of a man who was none of these things. Comrade Albert Woolson symbolizes all the great virtues of the common, ordinary citizen, the citizen who becomes a soldier and then returns to ordinary life." (dd)

Counting and Recounting the Civil War Dead

EPILOGUE

Poet and Civil War nurse Walt Whitman never got over the American Civil War.

In *Specimen Days*, a prose offering from 1892, Whitman remembered the dead. He called them *strayed*

dead, because they had left for the war and no one ever heard of them again. In many ways, it is the gentle outrage in Whitman's words that have framed the war for so many. One can imagine his messy, gray lion's mane of hair being pushed back by veined hands at the memory of what he described as "15,000 inhumed by strangers . . . 2,000 cover'd by sand and mud of Mississippi freshets, 3,000 carried away be caving-in of banks . . ."

Whitman's words grew less gentle as he confronted the stark reality of it all. He counted everyone for, to his mind, they were simply "the dead, the dead, the dead—*our* dead—or South or North, ours all." They "lay in bushes, low gullies, or on the sides of hills, in single graves, floating down the rivers, at the bottom of the sea."

Even now, in a digital age of impossible speed where killing the enemy has been refined to an art, Whitman's sorrowful words continue to remind his readers of something immortal, something that should not be forgotten. He called them *infinite dead*, and pointed out, "not only Northern dead leavening Southern soil—thousands, aye tens of thousands, of Southerners, crumble to-day in Northern earth . . . everywhere . . . these countless graves."

* * *

No matter how fervent the prayers, loved ones were not always protected. The ultimate aftermath of all Civil

ABOVE: *Numbers and Losses in the Civil War, 1861-65* (mg)

OPPOSITE: The statue *Fame* at Shiloh inscribes the count of the battle's dead:
  Brave of the brave,
    the twice five thousand men
  Who all that day stood in
    the battle's shock,
  Fame holds them dear, and
    with immortal pen
  Inscribes their names
    on the enduring rock. (cm)

War battles was death—a lot of death. For years, the toll of men (and maybe some women) who died as a result of the American Civil War stood rounded to 620,000: 360,222 from the North, 258,000 from the South. This number was accepted as a fact and rarely challenged.

So, from where exactly did the number come?

Two Union Army veterans who were passionate, albeit amateur, historians worked separately to arrive at a reasonable accounting of the Civil War dead. William F. Fox fought at Antietam, Chancellorsville, and Gettysburg and knew all too well the horrors of death on the battlefield and in camp. Beginning after the war, he researched every muster list, battlefield report, and pension record he could find in an effort to number the collective fatalities. In 1889, his treatise "Regimental Losses in the American Civil War, 1861-1865" presented an amazing amount of information to postwar Americans. Not only did Fox declare an aggregate death count, he informed his readers of such vital statistics as the average height (5 feet, 8 1/2 inches) and weight (143 1/2 pounds) of the average Union soldier.

Dissatisfied with other attempts to calculate the number of casualties in the war, Thomas Leonard Livermore compiled numbers of his own. His resultant *Numbers and Losses in the Civil War, 1861-65* remains a standard reference for historians. (mg)

Thomas Leonard Livermore, the other Union veteran, was not comfortable with Fox's figures, especially the ones for the Confederacy. Fox rounded the number of Southern deaths to 94,000, based on after-action reports from Confederate sources, but those sources were never claimed as accurate. Livermore reasoned that if the South had lost a proportionally equal number of soldiers to disease as the Union had, then the actual number of Confederate dead should be raised to at least 258,000. In 1900, he published his findings in the book *Numbers and Losses in the Civil War, 1861-65.*

And that was the end of that controversy for 110 years. Every historian—even the best known—used the Fox-Livermore figures in their work.

But in 2010, Dr. J. David Hacker, a history professor at Binghamton University who had an interest in historical statistics, took a look at the evidence. He used a little-known area of mathematics called the two-census method, an arcane area of knowledge involving the comparison of numbers in two census results to calculate a probable rate of mortality.

To explain briefly what this entails, war-related losses are estimated by comparing sex differences in mortality during the 1860s with sex differences in mortality in the 1850s and 1870s. The results indicate that the war was responsible for the deaths of about 750,000 men. Using less-conservative assumptions, the total may have been as high as 850,000.

Dr. Hacker was not quite the first to attempt this feat of mathematical magic. He was inspired by the previous work of Francis Amasa Walker, a beleaguered bean counter who was superintendent of the 1870 Census. Walker estimated the death toll even then to be as high as 850,000, but he knew it would be impossible to count the numbers exactly. Both armies lacked an adequate method of keeping track of their soldiers. There was no system in place to identify the dead, wounded, or missing in action. On both sides of the conflict, men simply disappeared. Hospital and prison records were as incomplete and inaccurate as battle records. Worst of all, there was nothing legally in place to notify a soldier's family of his eventual fate. With masses of soldiers buried as "unknowns," families were forced to infer the fate of a loved one from his failure to return home after the war ended in 1865.

Dr. J. David Hacker, professor of history at the University of Binghamton in upstate New York, used a form of statistical analysis to crunch battlefield numbers. (mg)

Unfortunately for Walker, his 1870 Census was held up to scrutiny by then-President Grant. Grant questioned its results and asked for recounts of several cities, including Philadelphia and New York. Walker argued mightily that his numbers were correct: the truth was that there were about one million men accounted for in the last census taken before the war who were now nowhere to be found.

Almost 150 years later, the situation gained the attention of Dr. Hacker, who began to search for those missing fellows. After all, beginning with the establishment of a national cemetery system after the battle of Gettysburg in 1863, the United States had moved towards a policy of identifying and burying, often reburying, the Union dead. By 1870, the remains of more than 300,000 soldiers had been located across the South and reinterred in national cemeteries. This was a very forceful statement of commitment on a national level to the men who had given their lives to the Civil War. It did not seem right to ask them to give up their names as well.

As bodies and names began to be recovered, more questions evolved concerning the actual numbers of the slain. The posy-war public began to demand some answers, but the only satisfaction they received was the promise from Col. Robert Scott, then an official of the War Department. "We will do these things better in

In Andersonville National Cemetery, a soldier with hat off and head bowed stands atop the Minnesota state memorial. (cm)

the next war," he said. This was cold comfort to those mourning their losses. The whole situation deserved more attention.

Dr. Hacker crunched his numbers, then crunched them again. The results were clear, it seemed. No matter how he looked at the situation, there were indeed 80,000 men in the 1860s census who were no longer around in 1870. Hacker's census-based method provided a more complete assessment of the war's human cost than previous methods. In addition to the number of men who died during their time of service, it provided an estimate of male mortality that included men who died from war-related factors between their discharge date and 1870. Hacker's new total for counting the Civil War dead was approximately 750,000 and may be as high as 850,000.

"If you want to argue that the conflict was very destructive, the 750,000 number could certainly suggest that," said Hacker in an article in *Binghamton Research*. "On the other hand, you could emphasize that neither army directly targeted the civilian population, that the number of civilian deaths was relatively low, and that most soldiers' deaths were not on the battlefield. Only when you add both sides' casualties, which we don't do for other wars, can you get to that total."

According to the new figures, one in five southern white men aged twenty to thirty four and one in nine northern white men of the same age died as a result of the Civil War.

Hacker is not without his detractors. But historians from Drew Gilpin Faust to James McPherson have welcomed Hacker's recounting, claiming that the result will be a deepened and expanded understanding of the war.

In the end, the controversy means that the topic matters to more than one person—and counting the Civil War dead ought to matter to many. The number is essential to understanding the war itself. Part of Confederate historiography claims that there were only twelve million Southerners against a juggernaut of twenty million Union soldiers. If new statistics prove correct, the argument of such numbers in the South loses a lot of its force.

Former general Grant noted, early on, one of the biggest obstacles to an accurate count. "There has always been a great conflict of opinion as to the number of troops engaged in every battle . . . the South magnifying the number of Union troops engaged and belittling their own." Not only were Confederate military records often inaccurate, many were destroyed in the fires when Richmond was finally taken in 1865.

In 1889, William Fox asked the readers of his book not to "grow impatient at these statistics. These numbers are not like ordinary figures." Each unit stands for "the pale, upturned face of a dead soldier. It is hard to realize the meaning of the figures . . . it is easy to imagine one man killed; or ten men killed; or, perhaps, a score of men killed . . . but even . . . the veteran is unable to comprehend the dire meaning of the one hundred thousand, whose every unit represents a soldier's bloody grave. The figures are too large."

David Hacker's new analysis suggests that the cost of the American Civil War was even higher than previously thought. This revised death count is greater than all American war deaths from all other conflicts combined.

No matter how you parse the data, though, the impact on American households was tremendous. "[W]ars have profound economic, demographic, and social costs," Hacker reminds us. "We're seeing at least 37,000 more widows . . . and 9,000 more orphans [than we realized before]. That's a profound social impact. . . ."

Looked at from this perspective, the shadow effect of American suffering extends much further than anyone realized.

Constructed while the war still waged, the Hazen Brigade monument represents one of the first attempts to memorialize the fallen on the field by the soldiers themselves. Today, it remains the oldest Civil War monument still standing in its original location. (cm)

Colonel Hazen's Monument

APPENDIX A

BY CHRISTOPHER KOLAKOWSKI

The Union Army of the Cumberland and Confederate Army of Tennessee fought the Battle of Stones River (or Murfreesboro) outside Murfreesboro, Tennessee, on the last day of 1862 and first two days of 1863. The battle was the Civil War's bloodiest by percentage of loss, with both sides leaving over 27% of their numbers on the field either killed, wounded, or missing.

For one unit, Stones River inspired a drive to mark the aftermath of battle in stone—which can still be seen today on the battlefield as the Hazen Monument.

Colonel William B. Hazen's brigade comprised the 6th Kentucky, 9th Indiana, 41st Ohio, and 110th Illinois, totaling approximately 1,500 men on December 31, 1862. Hazen, an Ohioan and Regular Army veteran, had commanded this brigade for virtually the entire year, including in the battles of Shiloh and Perryville. The former three regiments were veterans, while the Illinoisans were fighting their first battle.

At Stones River, Hazen's men deployed on the Army of the Cumberland's left as part of Brig. Gen. John M. Palmer's division. Their position included a four-acre circular cedar brake called the Round Forest. The wood stood on a slight incline, and Confederates faced it across an open field 700 yards eastward. Starting at dawn on December 31, Confederate attacks elsewhere gradually bent back the Federal line like a jackknife, with the Round Forest as its hinge; if Hazen's position fell, the entire Federal position would collapse.

During the afternoon, the Confederates hammered the Round Forest with repeated mass attacks. Between charges, Hazen recalled, "a murderous shower of shot and shell was rained from several directions upon this position." Shellbursts in

"Hell's Half-Acre" is now a scene of final repose and quiet contemplation. (cm)

the trees made splinters as deadly as shrapnel, and the din was so loud that men on both sides stuffed cotton in their ears. This concentrated fury earned the Round Forest the nickname "Hell's Half Acre." But as dusk fell, Hazen's men still held their line—the only part of the Federal army to do so that day.

After the battle, Hazen counted the high cost: 45 men killed, 335 wounded, and 29 missing, for a total of 409—29% of the brigade's strength. The survivors had saved the Army of the Cumberland while enduring a test unlike any they had experienced before. Desiring to honor his men, Hazen decided to build a monument next to the Round Forest as a centerpiece for a brigade cemetery.

The Hazen Monument, erected in the first months of 1863, is a box 10 feet square made of local limestone blocks about 1.6 feet thick. As the interior was filled with dirt, the men placed artillery shells and weapons from the battlefield inside; those items were discovered in 1985. The brigade's dead are buried around the monument under limestone markers, grouped by unit.

Inscriptions line all four sides, three of which pay tribute to the fighting on New Year's Eve 1862. The south face reads: "Hazen's Brigade/To the Memory of Its Soldiers Who Fell at Stones Rivers, Dec 31st 1862/ 'Their Faces Toward Heaven, Their Feet to the Foe.'"

The west face is more poetic, proclaiming "The blood of one third of its soldiers/Twice spilled in Tennessee/Crimsons the battle flag of the brigade/And

inspires to greater deeds." Below is a list of names of the brigade's dead officers from the battle.

The north face lists the brigade's regiments and commanders.

Significantly, the east face (facing the former Confederate positions) honors the officers of the brigade killed at Shiloh, thus making the Hazen Monument a marker to two battles. The east and west face inscriptions contain Col. Hazen's main message: his men carry a legacy forward and must live up to the example of those that have gone before.

Today the Hazen Monument is the oldest Civil War monument still in its original location, and is owned by the National Park Service as part of the Stones River National Battlefield.

Graves of the brigade's 45 killed cluster in neat rows around the monument. (cm)

The Confederate Dead of Franklin

APPENDIX B

BY ASHLEY WEBB

In the late afternoon of November 30, 1864, 30,000 Confederate troops, under General Hood's direction, made an attack on General Schofield's federal defenses in Franklin, Tennessee. With up to 10,000 casualties in the five-hour engagement, scores of dead and wounded were left on the battlefield or carried to make-shift field hospitals in and around the town of Franklin. The largest of these hospitals was Carnton Plantation, settled a little over a mile from what is now the hallowed ground of the battle.

Throughout the night and next day, more than 300 soldiers came to Carnton. Because of the house's close proximity to the battlefield, John and Carrie McGavock, owners of Carnton, played an integral role in assisting the wounded, as well as caring for the dead.

As line after line of Confederate soldiers rushed towards the entrenched Federal forces throughout the evening of November 30, the casualty list skyrocketed. The chaos was evident in Capt. William Gale's letter to his wife, dated January 14, 1865: "The fight was furious, and the carnage awful beyond anything I ever saw. . . . Charge after charge was made. As fast as one division was shattered and recoiled, another bravely went forward into the very jaws of death, and came back broken and bloody."

Even off the field at make-shift hospitals such as Carnton, chaos ensued. In the same letter to his wife, Capt. Gale commented on the conditions at Carnton upon his arrival the morning after the battle. "Every room was filled, every bed had two poor bleeding fellows, every spare space, niche and corner, under the stairs, in the hall, everywhere . . ." he wrote.

Blood soaked the floors where doctors cut off limbs and performed surgeries. When one soldier died, another took his place, and when the house "could hold no more, the yard was appropriated until the wounded and dead filled that, and all were [still] not yet provided for." One confederate soldier was lucky enough to garner a spot by the fire the night of the battle; another, who suffered from a leg wound, was not so lucky. "The house was overflowing with wounded . . ." he later wrote. "[I] spent the night on the ground in the yard."

Despite the chaos, Carrie McGavock and her family stayed calm. Carrie didn't sleep that fateful night, but she did what she could to ease the suffering by dispensing tea, coffee, and alcohol, "un-affrighted by the sight of blood, unawed by horrid wounds, [and] un-blanched by ghastly death. . . ." Her skirts trailed blood, and without

"There lies the Army of Tennessee," said historian Dan Davis the first time he visited McGavock Cemetery. (cm)

Since 1911, the McGavock Confederate Cemetery Corporation has continued to maintain and oversee the burial ground. (CP)

"Killed at Franklin" the cemetery's markers say. (CM)

the help of slaves—John had sent them to Alabama for the duration of the war—Carrie continued to nurse the injured with a few others. Unprepared for the massive influx of wounded, the doctors at Carnton ran out of bandages. Carrie ripped up "her old linen, then her towels and napkins, then her sheets and tablecloths, and then her husband's shirts and her own under garments" for the doctors' use.

Despite Carrie's and her household's ministrations, around 150 of the men brought to Carnton died that night. It is thought that three Confederate generals who were killed in the battle may have also been carried to Carnton—Patrick Cleburne, Hiram Granbury, and Otho Strahl—but some researchers think differently. One lieutenant remembers seeing the generals' bodies on the back porch with finely embroidered handkerchiefs over their faces.

The large number of men who did not make it through the night at Carnton does not compare to the number left on the field after the battle. Union forces headed toward Nashville on December 1, leaving in their wake several hundred dead Union soldiers, as well as around 1,700 Confederates. Lieutenant Edwin Rennolds walked the fields the day after the battle. "We found the dead lying so thick that we could have walked on them without stepping on the ground, a sight I never saw elsewhere," he remarked. Many of the dead were identified and placed in shallow graves throughout the battlefield. Hasty wooden plaques were placed with the bodies.

By 1866, however, many of the wooden markers had become unidentifiable, or had been removed and used as firewood. Additionally, the McGavock's neighbors were thinking of returning the battlefield to farmland, which raised the question concerning the remains from the battle. In response, the McGavocks donated two acres of their land to establish a Confederate cemetery for those killed at the battle of Franklin. They raised the funds with the support of the town to hire George Cuppett, a Confederate veteran, to oversee a few men, including his brother, in the exhumation and re-interment of around 1,500 Confederate soldiers to this cemetery, organized by state. Cuppett made careful note of each soldier's name, state, regiment, and final resting place in a small notebook, which Carrie kept throughout her life.

Built in 1826 by former Nashville mayor Randal McGavock, Carnton served as a field hospital during the battle of Franklin. The site was placed on the National Register of Historic Places in 1973. Today, it's open for tours and supported by private donations. (cm)

Not all soldiers buried in the McGavock Cemetery died at or as a result of the battle of Franklin. Several soldiers who were mortally wounded at the battle of Nashville are buried in the McGavock Cemetery, as well as a few soldiers who were killed in a skirmish in Franklin in 1863.

Johnson K. Duncan is the only general buried there; he died as a result of malaria in 1862, and at the request of his wife, his body was reburied at Carnton prior to 1870.

Additionally, one civilian is buried in the graveyard: Marcellus Cuppett, George Cuppett's younger brother, who passed away in 1866 while working on the re-interment project.

There are no Federal soldiers buried at Carnton, as most of those killed at the battle were moved to a national cemetery in Murfreesboro, Tennessee.

Despite the careful efforts of George Cuppett and the McGavocks, around 500 soldiers buried in the cemetery are still unidentified.

Although the last wounded soldier from the battle of Franklin left Carnton in July of 1865, the McGavocks continued care for the 1,500 dead left behind. Because many of the Confederate Army's officers and regimental commanders were injured, killed, or taken as prisoners at Franklin, the exact numbers and names of those taken to Carnton is still a mystery. Regardless, the bravery, selflessness, and generosity of the McGavocks has provided a lasting memorial to those who gave their lives to the Southern cause 150 years ago.

ASHLEY WEBB *is a freelance museums specialist in southwest Virginia and a contributor to Emerging Civil War.*

BETWEEN JULY 1864 AND AUGUST 1865, 2973
CONFEDERATE SOLDIERS WERE BURIED HERE
WITH KINDNESS AND RESPECT, BY JOHN W. JONES,
A RUNAWAY SLAVE. THEY HAVE REMAINED IN
THESE HALLOWED GROUNDS OF WOODLAWN
NATIONAL CEMETERY BY FAMILY CHOICE
BECAUSE OF THE HONORABLE WAY IN WHICH
THEY WERE LAID TO REST BY A CARING MAN.

The Dead of Hellmira

APPENDIX C

BY CHRIS MACKOWSKI

The frozen earth resisted his shovel, but John Jones was no stranger to hard work. He pitched in again, stabbing the ground and then driving the spade even further with his foot, prying loose one more chunk that he then heaved over his shoulder. The graves didn't come as easy as they had in the summer and fall, but there was now need for more of them than ever. Conditions in Elmira's prison camp had been bad to start with, he'd heard, but now that the weather had coldened so sharply, the Confederates being held there were dying off as many as ten a day.

Jones had been sexton of the Woodlawn cemetery since 1859. Before that, he'd worked as a laborer, a school janitor, and a church caretaker. Before that, he'd been a slave, owned by a family outside Leesburg, Virginia. In 1844, at the age of 27, he and two half-brothers had fled northward, following the Underground Railroad some three hundred miles to Elmira. Later, once established in Elmira, Jones worked as a "conductor" on the Railroad alongside whatever other jobs he'd had at the time.

The Elmira prison camp opened in July of 1864. The conditions were so bad, the camp soon earned the ignoble nickname "Hellmira." Of the 12,122 detainees held there during the camp's operation, 2,950 of them died—a death rate of 24.3%, says historian Michael Horigan in *Elmira: Death Camp of the North*. "During Elmira's 369 full days of existence," he writes, "the death rate averaged eight per day."

Compare that to Andersonville, the most notorious of the South's prison camps, where the death toll was 29%. "Yet even the most striking contrast between Andersonville and Elmira should be apparent even to the most casual observer," says Horigan. "Elmira, a city with excellent railroad connections, was located in a region where food, medicine, clothing, building materials, and fuel were in abundant supply. None of this could be said of Andersonville. Hence, Elmira became a symbol of death for different reasons."

Rather than ship the bodies of the Confederate dead home, Federal officials chose to bury the bodies adjacent to the city's Woodlawn Cemetery. Jones, who lived in a caretaker's house across the street from the cemetery, was responsible for overseeing the burials. He received $2.50 for each burial he performed. On each grave, he erected a hand-painted wooden marker, featuring the name of the deceased, and he kept records that included each Confederate's name, rank, company, and regiment, and

A monument in Woodlawn National Cemetery tells the story of escaped slave John Jones and the Confederate dead he tended. (cm)

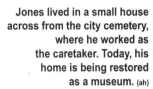

Jones lived in a small house across from the city cemetery, where he worked as the caretaker. Today, his home is being restored as a museum. (ah)

John Jones had escaped from a plantation in Leesburg, Virginia. Years later, the son of the plantation's overseer died as a prisoner at the Elmira prison camp. Jones arranged to have the body sent back to the family. (cchs)

CHRIS MACKOWSKI, PH.D., *is the editor-in-chief of Emerging Civil War.*

date of death. He also placed the information in a sealed glass bottle in each Confederate's coffin.

The graves stretch out in neat rows. Near the head of the plot stands a monument, erected by the U.D.C. in 1937, that features a bronze relief of a Confederate soldier who overlooks the Southern dead. "That statue depicted a healthy middle-aged man, fully clothed with hand in hand and good shoes—features atypical among Elmira inmates," points out historian Michael P. Gray in his book *The Business of Captivity: Elmira and Its Civil War Prison.*

Along the side of the plot stands a memorial to Jones, erected in 1997 by a group of high school students. "Confederate soldiers were buried here with kindness and respect by John W. Jones, a runaway slave," the monument says. "They have remained in these hallowed grounds of Woodlawn National Cemetery by family choice because of the honorable way in which they were laid to rest by a caring man."

There is also a memorial, erected in 1911, to commemorate the 44 Confederates and 17 Federals killed in a train accident in Shohola Township, in Pennsylvania's Pike County. Some 800 Confederate POWs were being transported to Elmira from Camp Lookout, Maryland, when their train collided with a coal train. The engineer, the brakeman, and two firemen also died in the crash. For forty-seven years, the dead lay interred in an unmarked grave next to the tracks where the accident took place., but the men were eventually disinterred and moved to Woodlawn.

More than 9,000 U.S. veterans and their family members are now buried at Woodlawn National Cemetery, which rests on ten and a half acres of land adjacent to the city's own Woodlawn Cemetery (from which the National Cemetery, formally established in 1877, takes its name).

In the city cemetery, on a knoll to the west that

A United Daughters of the Confederacy monument at the cemetery reads: "In memory of the Confederate soldiers in the War Between the States who died in Elmira prison and lie buried here." (cm)

The Shoholah monument (shown here in 1912 before the far field was added to the cemetery) has a plaque on one side commemorating the Confederate prisoners killed in a train accident on July 15, 1864; on the monument's reverse side, a plaque commemorates the Federal soldiers acting as guards who were also killed. (na)

overlooks the Confederate dead, Mark Twain's grave sits under the wide canopy of an old oak tree. Twain's wife, Olivia, came from Elmira, and the family often summered there. Twain wrote some of his most famous works, recollecting the lost days of the antebellum South, while living at the family's hilltop Quarry Farm.

What might Twain—who deserted from the Confederate army—have thought of the regimented rows of graves, Confederate POWs surrounded by Union soldiers—indeed, soldiers of many wars, intermingled with each other across the cemetery's ten-acre expanse?

"All war must be just the killing of strangers against whom you feel no personal animosity; strangers whom, in other circumstances, you would help if you found them in trouble, and who would help you if you needed it," Twain once wrote.

Here in Elmira, in this place of terrible memory where the prison camp once stood, a runaway slave buried the bodies of men who had fought to preserve a system that would have kept him enslaved. Jones saw strangers in trouble and helped them, when they needed it, to find rest.

The rows of markers stretched across the green lawn, surrounded by their fallen foes, spell out that story and call to us to remember.

APPENDIX D

BY BETSY DINGER AND EDWARD ALEXANDER

In the wake of the American Civil War, a New Jersey mother travelled to Virginia in vain attempt to find one of her fallen sons. The last time she saw her boy was as he hobbled back to the front lines in 1865, still nursing a leg wound suffered the previous year while carrying the flag in the Wilderness. She hired a guide to help scour the battlefields near Petersburg, and together they pinpointed the line of trenches the New Jersey Brigade assaulted on April 2. Comrades remembered their deceased lieutenant as the first one over the works that morning, shouting, "Come on, boys, come on!" But as he laid his hands on the enemy's cannon, the brave soldier fell. After the fighting died down, his friends hastily buried his body in a simple soldier's grave and crudely marked it with a board. After her visit, his disappointed mother could only report that her son's body remained missing on the battlefield where a farmer must have plowed it over.

It is likely that this soldier rests his final peace at Poplar Grove National Cemetery. Established in 1866, and today a unit of the Petersburg National Battlefield, the cemetery holds 6,181 burials of Union soldiers, many of them unknown, who died during the 292-day Siege of Petersburg. Prior to construction of the cemetery, the land hosted the winter campground of the 50th New York Engineers. The soldiers built a Gothic pine church during their stay and called it Poplar Grove, from which the cemetery's name is derived.

Between July 1866 and July 1869, burial teams searched farms, roadsides, and trenches in the surrounding areas to find the bodies of the fallen, ultimately covering 120 miles between Petersburg and Lynchburg. They reinterred these remains in the cemetery, in a circular fashion surrounding the center flagpole.

In 1868, David Macrae, a Scottish visitor touring the eastern United States, wandered for a while in the cemetery among the "melancholy forest of white headboards." Macrae was particularly moved by nearly 4000 unidentified graves. The wooden markers he saw were replaced in 1877 with upright white marble markers, similar to installations in other national cemeteries.

Every November for Veterans Day, the National Park Service holds a luminary event at Poplar Grove National Cemetery, with one light placed on every soldier's grave. (nps)

In 1933, the cemetery was transferred from the War Department to the National Park Service. At that

The flat headstones—and identities of the soldiers buried beneath them—eventually began to fall victim to erosion. (ea)

time, they took up the grave markers: the portions that contained the inscriptions were removed and replaced over the grave; the bottom sections of the markers were sold off as excess property to a man who used it to build a house just of Petersburg. Referred to locally as the "Tombstone House" the structure was once voted the "eeriest house in America" by an architectural digest.

The markers, originally altered as a money-saving feature, are now worn or unreadable due to maintenance and the elements. The cemetery no longer retains its nineteenth century appearance. But despite these unflattering changes to the physical layout, these nine acres still constitute sacred ground, and for nearly 150 years families continue to visit the graves.

In 1868 ,the mother of Theodore Tenney, killed at the Battle of Five Forks, traveled from Ohio to see the grave of her younger son. Her older son, Lumen, who had been with his brother when he was killed, recorded, "We found Theodore's grave very pleasantly situated in the national cemetery near Petersburg. Everything seemed very satisfactory to Ma. We got flower and put on the grave. . . . " The Tenney family's sense of loss must have been tempered by knowing where Theodore rested, in grave #101, and by knowing that his grave would be cared for in perpetuity.

As part of the commitment to care for the cemetery, beginning in late 2015, the National Park Service will undertake a major rehabilitation project to return

In 1934, Oswald Young bought more than 2,200 of Poplar Grove's disassembled tombstones and built a house out of them not far from the cemetery. Today, the "Tombstone House," as it's called locally, remains a private residence. (cm)

Poplar Grove National Cemetery to its post Civil War appearance. A key feature of the project will be to replace the existing but damaged grave markers with new upright white marble markers. Visitors will be able to see the cemetery as it would have looked before the 1933 alteration. Improvements to the cemetery will allow future visitors to Theodore Tenney's grave, as well as all the other graves, to experience Poplar Grove as it was originally intended, as a place where the graves of the dead will "be kept sacred forever."

BETSY DINGER *is a park ranger at Petersburg National Battlefield and Poplar Grove National Cemetery.*
EDWARD ALEXNDER, *a historical interpreter at Pamplin Historical Park in Petersburg, is a regular contributor to Emerging Civil War.*

AN ACT

TO ESTABLISH AND TO PROTECT NATIONAL CEMETERIES.

APPROVED FEBRUARY 22, 1867.

* * *

Section 3.

And be it further enacted, That any person who shall willfully destroy, mutilate, deface, injure, or remove any monument, gravestone, or other structure, or shall willfully destroy, cut, break, injure, or remove any tree, shrub, or plant within the limits of any of said National Cemeteries, shall be deemed guilty of a misdemeanor, and upon conviction thereof before any District or Circuit Court of the United States within any State or District where any of said National Cemeteries are situated, shall be liable to a fine of not less than twenty-five nor more than one hundred dollars or to imprisonment of not less than fifteen nor more than sixty days, according to the nature and aggravation of the offense. And the Superintendent in charge of any National Cemetery is hereby authorized to arrest forthwith any person engaged in committing any misdemeanor herein prohibited, and to bring such person before any United States Commissioner or Judge of any District or Circuit Court of the United States, within any State or District where any of said Cemeteries are situated, for the purpose of holding said person to answer for said misdemeanor, and then and there make complaint in due form.

According to the National Park Service, "Nationwide, 54% of the number of re-interred [Civil War soldiers] are classified as 'unknown.' At Vicksburg National Cemetery, 75% of the Civil War dead are listed as unknowns, while at Salisbury (N.C.) National Cemetery, 99% of the 12,126 Federal soldiers interred are listed as unidentified." (cm)

Return Visit to Vicksburg
APPENDIX E
BY MATT ATKINSON

On April 12, 1880, a carriage proceeded north from Vicksburg along a dirt road at the base of the river bluffs. After a few miles, a large stone arch came into view, marking the entrance to Vicksburg National Cemetery. The occupants noted the inscription:

> Here Rest In Peace 16,600 Citizens,
> Who Died For Their Country,
> In The Years 1861 To 1865.

Passing through the gate, the group espied a group of graves to their left denoting the officer's circle. Water sprayed from the top of cannon in the center, made possible by a gravity-fed water pipe from atop the hillside.

As the carriage started up the switchback road leading to the top of the bluff, small white stones, thousands of them, began to appear in view, all arranged in sweeping arches along terraces hand dug from the hillside. The carriage continued to roll along the hedgerow-lined avenue as the occupants marveled at the various trees and flowers.

The distinguished visitors that day had no way to know that the very existence of a National Cemetery in Vicksburg was in itself, miraculous. Unlike at Gettysburg after the battle there, the Federal government did not make any effort to collect the Vicksburg dead until after the conclusion of the war. The military campaigns to capture the Hill City had spanned more than a year, from 1862 to 1863, and had left corpses from the campsites across the river in Louisiana to the battlefields of Mississippi. A Union garrison, consisting primarily of United States Colored Troops, remained in Vicksburg until 1870.

In 1866, Col. James F. Rushing had visited the area to inspect the battlefields and burial sites. He found the condition of the dead "more deplorable than any post I have visited." Rushing concluded that an estimated 8,000 Union dead lay on the Mississippi side of the river and another 2,000 on the Louisiana side. He estimated another 5,000 burials on outlying battlefields such as Chickasaw Bayou, Port Gibson, Raymond, Jackson, Champion Hill, and Big Black River.

The Colonel urged the War Department to acquire suitable ground for a cemetery. The government complied on August 6, 1866, purchasing forty acres north of the city for $9,000.

In 1867, work parties began to exhume the dead. Despite a labor force of 260 workers, internments averaged only sixteen a day. The problem lay in that the ground selected for the cemetery was a hill and literally had to be leveled off by hand. Therefore, the reburial process did not begin in earnest until 1868.

The task of retrieving the dead proved daunting. Not

only did the superintendents of exhumations have a wide territory to cover, in many cases they also faced a hostile populace. Government agents reported that property owners planted crops on the graves, removed headboards, and sometimes denied any existence of soldiers' remains. Local lore states that poor people sometimes burned the headboards for firewood. In 1868, George Macy described how local farmer Adam Lynd had intentionally denied any knowledge of graves on his property. Subsequently, Lynd "wantonly Plowed over our Union dead, scattering the bones in every direction." Macy reported that his work detail later recovered thirty-seven bodies from the farm. An ambrotype of a mother and child were found in one soldier's grave, a mere fifteen yards from the Confederate lines. "Certainly his grave should have been respected," Macy wrote, "but it was not."

Vicksburg National Cemetery rolls across 116 acres of high bluffs that overlook the Mississippi River. (loc)

The occupants of the carriage that day in 1880 may not have known the obstacles in the construction, but one man in particular certainly knew the price. Seventeen years before, his decisions had led to many a soldier's death. And now, as he gazed out on the rows of graves, where did his thoughts turn?

By August, 1868, 15,595 internments had been made. The graves comprised 3,193 whites and 130 blacks among the known soldiers; 6,589 whites and 5,458 blacks remained unknown. Although the soldiers served on the same side, the cemetery avenue separated the white and black sections.

By 1880, 17,077 dead were interred there, with a staggering 12,909 comprising the unknown. An estimated 5,000 Confederate dead lie only a few miles away in the city cemetery.

The carriage turned a corner, and before the occupants rose a large Indian Mound and, atop the crest, an obelisk monument. The monument had originally stood upon the site where the surrender interview had taken place. Vandalism had forced its removal to the cemetery for safekeeping. In the carriage, the gray-haired gentleman's thoughts on this piece of granite, a tribute to one of his greatest achievements, went unrecorded also.

The carriage stopped and the party climbed out

to walk the grounds. All the laborers in the cemetery seemed captivated by the gentleman. He walked the rows of graves, staring down at the names or, in many cases, mere numbers. Did he recognize any? Did he know any of their stories?

During the siege of Vicksburg, the fighting along the Halls Ferry Road was nip and tuck. On the night of June 25, the 33rd Wisconsin tried to advance their siege approach closer to the Confederate line. In the subsequent firefight, Fred Taylor and William Dunbar suffered wounds to the thigh and hand respectively. On the night of June 30, Taylor passed away. A detail of six men retrieved his body from the hospital and buried Taylor on a "high ridge near a small oak tree in the rear of Vicksburg." On July 3, Dunbar joined Taylor under the same tree. As the distinguished gentleman walked through the rows, he might have noticed that when the bodies were exhumed, these two comrades were reinterred side by side in the National Cemetery in graves 5263 and 5264.

Although referred to as the "Indian mound," a raised area in the cemetery is merely an eroded hill. Archeological work done in the area in the 1960s found no traces of Native American artifacts. (loc)

Perhaps the visitor took note of the unusual grave of E. C. D. Robbins. He enlisted in 17th Illinois Infantry and rose from private to first lieutenant. On May 21, 1864, he accepted a promotion in the 53rd United States Colored Infantry to the rank of captain. On October 15, 1864, Robbins "committed suicide by shooting himself through the head." Two tombstones mark the grave of Robbins, numbers 4267 and 4305. One is a generic government stone; the other was placed by friends with the inscription "resurgam" that translates "I shall rise again."

A further walk brought the gentleman to the resting site of Henry Cady, grave 2735. "Little Cady," as one soldier remembered him, "was universally acknowledged to be the best boy in the Comp'y. . . ." Cady died on July 1. "There was not one in the Comp'y who would not do any thing for him. We all loved him dearly, and now he is taken from us. The boys all mourn for him."

Later, the carriage returned to the wharf ,and the passengers climbed aboard the steamboat. "There was a time when your presence here was less welcome than it is to-day," a former antagonist had reminded him earlier.

"I am glad that the conflict is over," the old general replied, "never again to be resumed, and that it left us united."

Cigar clinched in his mouth, he took one last gaze at the city that had cost so many lives.

MATT ATKINSON *is a ranger/ historian with Gettysburg National Military Park and a former ranger/historian at Vicksburg National Military Park.*

Suggested Reading

THE AFTERMATH OF BATTLE

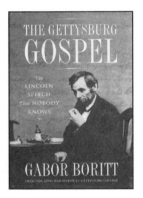

The Gettysburg Gospel: The Lincoln Speech That Nobody Knows
Gabor Boritt
Simon & Schuster (2006)
ISBN: 978-0-7432-8820-0

Gabor Boritt's book is filled with quotes and first-person accounts of the long, dark night that was the aftermath of the battle itself, but his most important contribution is to put the Gettysburg Address back into the context of the small town of Gettysburg and of the war itself. Lincoln's short, elegant offering at the Gettysburg Cemetery was meant as an explanation of why the horror of war must continue. As simple as that may sound, the job of convincing a nation that Union and Emancipation were worthy causes was one that only a leader like Abraham Lincoln could accomplish.

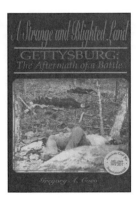

A Strange and Blighted Land
Gregory A. Coco
Thomas (1995)
ISBN-13: 978-1577470410

Gregory Coco is the best-known historian who's written about the aftermath of the battle of Gettysburg. His numerous books, including *Wasted Valor: The Confederate Dead at Gettysburg* and both *Killed In Action* volumes, are essential to anyone wondering about the aftermath of Gettysburg. Not only did this battle touch both the Union and Confederate armies, it touched the state of Pennsylvania, the county of Adams, and the town of Gettysburg. Coco's work is detailed, but very readable. Unfortunately, the publisher has made the book unnecessarily difficult to find.

Learning from the Wounded: The Civil War and the Rise
of American Medical Science
Shauna Devine
University of North Carolina Press (2014)
ISBN: 978-1-4696-1155-6

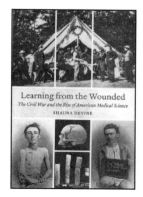

The history of medicine is incomplete without acknowledging
its debt to the medical advances made during the American
Civil War. This neglected chapter of war history is finally
beginning to be recognized, and Devine's book makes great
strides in that direction. The emphasis on the importance of
the Army Medical Museum alone gives this volume a place
on any complete Civil War bookshelf.

This Republic of Suffering: Death and the American Civil War
Drew Gilpin Faust
Alfred A. Knopf (2008)
ISBN: 978-0-375-40404-7

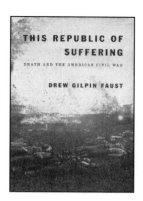

Gilpin Faust's book provides an insightful study of the
changes in attitude toward death in general and war death
in particular in mid-19th century America. Those who lived
during the time of the Civil War continued their lives with
grief and loss, yet they still brought America into a new age
of commerce, technology, and international power. Just what
made this generation so exceptional is a question historians
continue to ponder.

Antietam: The Photgraphic Legacy of America's Bloodiest Day
William Frassanito
Scribner (1978)
ISBN-13: 978-0684156590

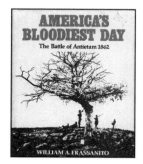

Frassanito's seminal work on Civil War photography is at its
best in his examination of Gardner's Antietam photography.
He explains the background of the photos and matches each
one with its modern location. A visitor can literally travel the
battlefield with book in hand to better understand Gardner's
visit to the field—and gain a new appreciation for it today, too.

Burying the Dead But Not the Past:
Ladies Memorial Associations & the Lost Cause
Caroline E. Janney
University of North Carolina Press (2008)
ISBN: 978-0-8078-3176-2

One of the difficulties of fairly balancing a book that depends on official records is the lack of those records for one side. This is the case for the Confederacy, which lost much of its valuable information to fire and other calamity during and after the war. Janney's valuable contributions to the Southern side of the record may be found in this book, and in her newer *Remembering the Civil War: Reunion and the Limits of Reconciliation.*

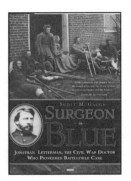

Surgeon in Blue: Jonathan Letterman, the Civil War Doctor
Who Pioneered Battlefield Care
Scott McGaugh
Arcade Publishing (2013)
ISBN: 978-1-61145-839-8

McGaugh's excellent biography of Dr. Jonathan Letterman is the only book on this interesting and often-neglected figure. Many of the innovations Letterman developed for the battlefield and for the military medical corps are still in use today. This book is one of the first in what should prove to be a fruitful line of inquiry.

Second Only to Grant: Quartermaster General
Montgomery C. Meigs
David W. Miller
White Mane Books (2000)
ISBN: 1-57249-212-0

The office of Quartermaster General was narrowly defined prior to the war, but under Meig's capable hands, it was enlarged to include doctors, medicine, caskets, regulations concerning the burial of the dead, and the creation of military cemeteries. These new topics examined together create a better and more complete understanding of the Civil War.

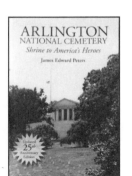

Arlington National Cemetery: Shrine to America's Heroes
James Edward Peters
Woodbine House (2008)
ISBN-13: 978-1-890627-92-8

Peters delves into the stories behind the names inscribed on the graves to offer an excellent history of the cemetery and the people enshrined there. Although he overlooks some notables—Jonathan Letterman is omitted entirely, for instance—the book is still an excellent collection of profiles and histories.

Memoranda During the Civil War: Civil War Journals,
1863-1865
Walt Whitman
Dover Publications (2010)
ISBN: 978-0-486-47641-4

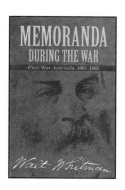

It is never a good idea to overlook Walt Whitman when examining the human aspect of the Civil War. From fighting bureaucracies to bedside nursing, Whitman's hand is as sure as his pen. His quote, "The real war will never get in the books," is a challenge worth taking up.

Turned Inside Out: Recollections of a Private Soldier
in the Army of the Potomac
Frank Wilkeson
University of Nebraska Press (1997)
ISBN: 008032-9799-8

In the words of Private Wilkeson, who served as an artillerist in several different companies in the Army of the Potomac, the reader goes beyond a simple daily accounting of life in the Union army. Wilkeson is a first-rate writer, and he is brutally honest in his descriptions of the type of warfare that brought down so many of his fellow men. He examines pain, fear, and depression first hand. Later editing does not attempt to make these feelings any less terrifying. Here is the aftermath of battle from the pen of one who saw many aftermaths.

. . . and if you have time:

- *Hospital Sketches* by Louisa May Alcott
- *Ambrose Bierce's Civil War* by Ambrose Bierce
- *These Honored Dead: How the Story of Gettysburg Shaped American Memory* by Thomas A. Desjardin
- *Gone For a Soldier: The Civil War Memoirs of Private Alfred Bellard* edited by David Herbert Donald.
- *Marrow of Tragedy: The Health Crisis of the American Civil War* by Margaret Humphries
- *The Sacred Remains: American Attitudes Toward Death, 1799-1883* by Gary Laderman
- *The Vacant Chair: The Northern Soldier Leaves Home* by Reid Mitchell
- *Beautiful Death: Art of the Cemetery* by David Robinson
- *Awaiting the Heavenly Country: The Civil War and America's Culture of Death* by Mark Shantz

About the Author

Meg (Thompson) Groeling, a contributing writer at Emerging Civil War, explores subjects beyond the battlefield—such as personalities, politics, and practices that affected the men who did the fighting. Aside from *The Aftermath of Battle*, she has also written *First Fallen: The Life and Times of Colonel Elmer Ellsworth*, the only biography written about Ellsworth since Ruth Painter Randall's, published in 1960. Meg teaches math at Brownell Middle School, named for E. E. Brownell, a California educator who was named for Colonel Elmer Ellsworth and is related to Corporal Francis Brownell, the man who shot the man who killed Ellsworth.

Meg's undergraduate degree in Liberal Studies with a minor in American History was from California State University, Long Beach. She is finishing her masters degree in History, with a Civil War emphasis.